Praise for

"Reading *Women Rise Up* felt like the first time in thousands of years of sacred storytelling, women are finally being believed. Accessible and relatable, rich and nuanced, Katey speaks the truth of the abuse, oppression, and erasure women have endured in the stories told about us. Faithful to the best of hermeneutical practices, she weaves contextual biblical stories of women with urgent concerns of today's global women so we can benefit from the wisdom and solidarity of our sisterhood through the ages. This book transforms stories of women that have been used to oppress, into ones that liberate—I'm here for it."

Cindy Brandt, author of *Parenting Forward*

"*Women Rise Up* is a thoroughly engaging book that holds stories of women in the Bible side-by-side with current issues facing women today. Katey Zeh takes the Bible seriously—so seriously that she is willing to acknowledge its complexity and ambiguity while looking to it for wisdom. She brings biblical stories and issues of women's health together and invites readers to do the same. Zeh's approach does not produce a list of 'musts' and 'shouldn'ts,' but rather a model of intelligent faithfulness attentive to the full humanity of women."

Rev. Dr. Shannon Craigo-Snell, Professor of Theology, Louisville Presbyterian Theological Seminary

"This is the book the Church needs for such a time as this. Katey Zeh has created a book that is moving, convicting, and empowering. It is an invaluable resource for pastors, small groups, women, and men who yearn for liberation. For far too long, the Church has treated the women in these Biblical stories as interesting side notes at best; and antagonistic instruments of manipulation at worst. No more! Drawing on her own experience as a mother, an advocate for women's health within the global church, and the best of modern scholarship; Zeh has reclaimed these stories with forcefulness, boldness, and a remarkable amount of vulnerability."

Rev. Robb McCoy, Pastor of Two Rivers United Methodist Church, Rock Island, Illinois, Co-Producer of *The Pulpit Fiction Podcast*

"I don't know anyone who more seamlessly marries her scriptural imagination with an activist sensibility than Katey Zeh. She is a reliable, skilled, and (thanks to be God) altogether human teacher who is not afraid to trouble the waters of some of our most beloved (and forgotten) readings of biblical women - and their enduring witness in our modern lives. If you are looking for an easy bake women's book study, you won't find it here. But if you dare to go where few have willingly gone into this study of what it means to be a female follower of God, you will come out the other side just as Zeh hoped: more resilient, more compassionate, and better able to rise up in the face of injustices near and far. I recommend this book to any girl beginning to wonder what relevancy the biblical stories have in her life - and any pastor, counselor, parent, or mentor who cares enough to walk into the complexity with her."

Erin Lane, author of *Lessons in Belonging*

"Katey Zeh weaves together familiar biblical stories with her personal story. Giving birth, everyday family life, trying to live in solidarity in unjust times are all themes with biblical echo. Lots of people will resonate with her direct, accessible approach to women rising up."

Dr. Mary E. Hunt, Co-Founder of
The Women's Alliance for Theology, Ethics, and Ritual

"Katey Zeh has embarked upon a sober, brave accounting of the Bible's stories of women. Even as she notes their rarity among the more well-known stories of male characters, she finds in these women the kind of strength and compassion that might fuel our struggles for justice today. This book is recommended reading for those who hope for a better world, and I'm grateful to her for writing it."

Jim Winkler, President of the National Council of Churches

"*Women Rise Up* will inspire you with its thoughtful and eloquent explorations of women in biblical stories—some familiar; some less so—braided with contemporary stories of women the world over. If you have felt stifled by the narratives of womanhood offered to you by religious texts and communities, Katey Zeh's words will bring you a fresh infusion of oxygen, and will inspire you to press on, to reach out, and to rise up."

Rachel Marie Stone, author of *Birthing Hope*

"Part memoir, part bible study - in this volume, Katey Zeh walks the reader through familiar bible stories, offering rich food for thought for women seeking spiritual guidance and reflection."

Rev. Dr. Rebecca Todd Peters, author of *Trust Women*

"Stories have the power to change lives and shift political and cultural ideologies. When we excavate the untold stories or the invisible stories that have been pushed to the margins of the margins and silenced, we not only unearth, literally, our own lifeblood, but we also re-story ourselves in deeply embodied ways. Katey Zeh does this very thing of re-storying the women of the Bible in ways that bring together today's pressing social concerns of reproductive justice and visibilizing the stories that have been excised and silenced from the Tradition. The work of re-storying is also the work of re-telling our own stories in ways that bring to life what has been been buried by the dominant culture."

Dr. Robyn Henderson-Espinoza, Theologian and Activist

Published by The FAR Press

An imprint of Blaise Publications

Cleveland, Ohio

www.thefarpress.com

Printed in the United States of America

Library of Congress Cataloging-in-Publication-Data

Name: Zeh, Katey author.

Title: Women Rise Up

Description: Cleveland: The FAR Press [2019]

Identifiers: ISBN 978-0-9989675-5-4

Women Rise Up

Sacred Stories of Resistance for Today's Revolution

Women Rise Up

Sacred Stories of Resistance for Today's Revolution

Katey Zeh

Contents

Acknowledgments

This book has been several years in the making. You could call it a long gestation. First, I want to thank my publisher Gina Messina for believing in my vision for this book before I even began writing it. She has been affirming, patient, and encouraging throughout the entire process.

Many of my early essays were inspired by the wonderful women and men with whom I worked on the issue of maternal health advocacy: Linda Bales Todd, Katie Kraft, Jan Todd, Courtney Fowler, Sharon Ritter, Jessie Cunningham, Mary Larson, Vanessa Wilson, Nancy Brown, Gina Gile, Theresa Moxley, Robb McCoy, and Cynthia Rives. Thanks to all of you for modeling gracious leadership and for your tireless advocacy for women and girls.

Rosie Molinary, Erin Lane, and Margaret Brunson were thought partners and coaches who talked me through the process of crafting a book proposal and getting through writing the first draft. Thank you for helping me take that daunting first step.

To the people of Pullen Church who recognized my call to ordained ministry in large part because of this book, I am so grateful for your support and affirmation. I'm especially grateful to Brian Crisp, Cathy Tamsberg, and Nancy Petty for their willingness to journey alongside me in this work.

I couldn't have done this without the tremendous support of my family. My mother Marty cared for our infant daughter while I wrote my first draft. Thank you, Nana!

To my husband Matt and my daughter Samantha: thank you for making life beautiful, hope-filled, and joyous. You give me the strength to carry this work forward with faith that the world can become a kinder, more compassionate place.

Lastly, to my grandmother Honey: I'll bet you never expected a book like this from me. I hope I make you proud.

Introduction

As a child I loved church. I know that's an odd thing to say, but it's the truth. Sunday was my favorite day of the week. But it wasn't always so.

Unlike a lot of kids I knew, my parents didn't drag my brothers and me to worship every week. In fact, I don't think I even stepped inside a church until I was eight years old. My grandmother "Honey" was the one who first invited me. She'd been raised in the Alabama fire-and-brimstone kind of way, which had kept her out of church for most of her adult life. But she'd never lost her faith.

For my birthday one year Honey had bought me an illustrated children's Bible, the kind with scant words and full-page cartoon drawings. Admittedly, a Bible wasn't at the top of my wish list. I couldn't understand why she'd gifted me a book instead of a Barbie.

Not long after that my grandmother received the devastating diagnosis that she had advanced lung cancer. The sickness quickly spread to her brain. That was when she found her way back to church. She opted for a small Methodist congregation not far from her house. The theology was conservative, but the pastor was a kind, gentle man with a surprisingly wicked sense of humor. The only sermon of his I can remember was the one he preached at her funeral. My grandmother had been an avid golfer, and a skilled one to boot, and he spoke of her life as a round of golf. Even as a child I remember being struck by how personal the pastor's eulogy was and how he'd taken great care in getting to know her in such a short period of time.

My young heart ached for just one more Sunday together. I was devastated by her death. And I had no one to take me to church anymore.

Honey had a small, hardback book about Jesus that she kept next to the rose-colored recliner in her bedroom. After she died, I asked my grandfather if I could keep it. I pored over its pages night after night, fascinated by the stories of Jesus's life, ministry, and death. Reading it helped me feel connected to my grandmother, but it also opened up a world of sacred stories I had not known.

As I entered adolescence, I found my way back to church. Finally, I was old enough to participate in youth group on Sunday nights, and eventually I began attending morning services too. Soon I was signing up for weekly Bible study, teaching Sunday school, and singing in the praise band. Church became everything to me. Church was home.

All of this church-going made me feel quite devout and pious. I'd started memorizing Scripture, so I could recite verses impressively. I read my neon-colored Teen Study Bible almost daily, highlighting favorite passages in neon-colored ink, and took notes in my prayer journal about what I read. I thought I knew the sacred stories well.

As it turns out, I knew only certain stories. Men's stories, to be exact.

Women's stories in the Bible were nowhere to be found on Sunday mornings. Despite all the services and studies I attended, women were seldom mentioned and were even more seldom a focus of the stories told and lessons taught. Like a frame holding a picture, the roles biblical women played were treated as ancillary to the "real" story. You know, the one involving all of those men.

I went along with this male-dominated storyline without comment or complaint for quite some time because, to be honest, it never occurred to me that women had been left out. I didn't know what I didn't know. I'd never witnessed a woman preaching from the pulpit either. How could I know that it was in the realm of possibility if I'd never seen it modeled for me?

There were a few rare exceptions when women were talked about at length in church, but it was never for good reasons. I came to expect that whenever a woman was mentioned in the sermon, she was going to wreak havoc: Eve would eat. Delilah would tempt. Martha would complain. If women are responsible for so much sinning, I thought, no wonder Paul tells us all to be silent in church.

As I grew into my later teen years, the messages about a woman's place became much more explicit. My role, I was told by youth leaders, was to be pursued by a "godly man," to be passive and wait for him to make things happen and to be my leader. To be a good Christian woman I needed to shut up, cover up, and shape up. After years of this I eventually got fed up.

Though at the time I didn't have the precise language to articulate it, I tried to speak up about my misgivings when I could. How could women be to blame for all the evils of the world? There was no way God created women just to be the antagonists in every man's story.

Once, sitting in a women's Bible study on Genesis and gender roles, I pointed out that there were two different accounts of creation, and that in our discussion we'd skipped right over the one in which women and men were made at the same time and in the image of God. Didn't this mean we were created equally? Didn't this mean we held the same worth? The study leader brushed off my question and continued on with her prepared lesson, visibly perturbed by my interjection. I never went back to that Bible study group.

Another time the issue of women's ordination came up in an evangelical women's gathering I attended. I was in high school at the time, and the leaders were college students. I'll never forget the severe tongue-lashing I got from one of them, though just a few years older than me, who insisted that it was against God's will for a woman to be ordained—and that a woman shouldn't even hold public office. I was stunned and heartsick. I felt betrayed by the other women in the room who had remained silent.

I didn't know how to reconcile my love of the church with these teachings that felt so unfair, so wrong at a gut level. For a while my strategy was to bypass these problematic biblical texts as much as I could. If I couldn't ask my questions freely, then I wanted to forget about them. Repression didn't work; it only made me resentful, even angry. Eventually I quit the Bible studies that I'd once attended so religiously. I began searching for passages on my own that might counter these negative ideas about what it meant to be a woman. I delved into the text, reading and re-reading entire books of the Bible I'd never studied carefully. I was surprised to see how often women appeared, at times nominally but at other times substantially. The Bible was peppered with all kinds of stories about women—I had just never heard about them in church.

Some stories were almost impossible to read—stories of violence endured and violence inflicted, stories of oppression suffered and oppression imposed. These are the kinds of stories that biblical scholar Phyllis Trible appropriately refers to as "texts of terror." There, among the pages of a book that I'd believed to be inspired by God, were women who had been raped, mutilated, used, coerced, and silenced. How could I make sense of these injustices committed against women in the name of God? How could there be any redemption in these "sacred" stories? What was there to call holy anymore?

Maybe you know what I'm talking about. You've encountered a biblical text that raises hard questions that frankly no one wants to hear, much less discuss thoughtfully. Maybe it's the text about God telling Eve after the fall that she will have pain in childbearing. Or the brutal rape of Tamar. Or the admonition that wives should submit to their husbands. Or any text in which women are dehumanized and devalued simply for being women. Maybe you have been able to muster up the strength to wrestle with these texts. Or maybe like me you've encountered one too many passages that make you want to close the so-called good book permanently. Maybe you've done just that. Enough. No more.

I distinctly remember once sitting in a theology class when someone brought up the text from 1 Corinthians 14 that says women are to be silent in church, and I completely shut down. I couldn't even participate in the discussion. I couldn't engage one more time the same old conversation that would question my standing in the eyes of God. It was too exhausting for me to put up with that anymore.

Like my grandmother whose faith in God was steadfast even when her faith in church wavered, these struggles I had with the Bible—and in conversations about the Bible—didn't extinguish my quest for knowing the divine. I studied theology in college and then enrolled in divinity school. I began to discern a call that would take me beyond the walls of the academy and the church to advocate for gender justice in the world.

After graduating from divinity school I moved to Washington, D.C. to work full-time in faith-based advocacy for women and girls. There were days when confronting the realities of human trafficking, maternal mortality, child marriage, and poverty felt like too much to bear. It overwhelmed me, and I began to doubt my ability to continue on in this line of work. If I couldn't muster up enough hope to keep myself going each day, how could I possibly convince anyone else to join me in the movement for gender justice?

A lot of my prayers those days sounded like, "Come on, God! Help me out here." I was desperate for some good news, but I was scared to look for it in the Bible. That book had let me down in major ways. Could God somehow crack open the Scriptures to bring a message of hope for women and girls amongst these texts of terror and oppression?

I began my hopeful search by returning to the story of creation. Despite the many struggles I had with some sacred texts, I still believed at my core that what I'd read at the beginning of Genesis so many years earlier was still true: that God created all of us, no matter our gender identity, in the imago dei (image of God) with equal sacred worth. We are all beloved beings made in the likeness of the divine and born with innate sacred worth. Gender injustice, in all its forms both past and present, was simply evidence that the world was askew and not as it should be.

At the same time I had to acknowledge the unfiltered reality of the biblical text: women are excluded, unnamed, and reduced to the roles they play in the lives of men. These passages are the ones to which men turn in order keep women in their place, to limit their gifts, and to prevent them from accessing power. People use these texts to justify abuses in women's interpersonal relationships, unfair treatment and policies in their communities and countries, and the omission of women in positions of influence, both in the church and beyond.

The challenge for me was learning to hold the uncomfortable space of paradoxical truths—that indeed, some people will always use sacred texts to justify women's marginalization and oppression, but the Bible can also be a source of our collective liberation.

I wrote this book because I am hungry for hope that speaks to the work of the gender justice needed today. I yearn for stories of resilience, of women overcoming systems of oppression who found ways to survive and even thrive despite the constant threats to their bodies, their humanity, and their livelihood. I am desperate for the Spirit to breathe new life into these ancient stories that will give us the strength to carry this legacy forward.

As I began to explore these sacred stories, I was mindful that the issues of injustice, violence, and abuse women faced long ago are not unlike the ones women and girls suffer from today. They happen everywhere, not only in distant places around the world but also in our local communities, neighborhoods, houses of worship, and homes. As people of faith, we are called to respond, to advocate, and to create change.

This book is an exploration and an affirmation of women's lives—yours and mine, ancient and new, near and distant. It is an invitation to connect, commune, and converse with the foremothers of our faith. These women are complex figures deserving of our attention, sometimes our admiration, and other times our critique. Oftentimes all three at once.

Throughout these pages I offer what these Scriptures mean to me and what I believe they have to offer us today in our personal faith journeys and in our movements for justice. My hope is that you will feel invited to dialogue and converse with them in your own ways. From time to time, you may disagree entirely with my reading of certain Scriptures. Not only is that acceptable, but I highly encourage it!

As you read, study, and struggle with hard questions about these stories from the Bible, I pray that you will encounter these women in new ways. I pray that their voices, their decisions, and their actions will speak to you from these ancient pages. They have much to teach us.

Genesis 16:1-16

Now Sarai, Abram's wife, bore him no children. She had an Egyptian slave-girl whose name was Hagar, and Sarai said to Abram, "You see that the Lord has prevented me from bearing children; go in to my slave-girl; it may be that I shall obtain children by her." And Abram listened to the voice of Sarai. So, after Abram had lived ten years in the land of Canaan, Sarai, Abram's wife, took Hagar the Egyptian, her slave-girl, and gave her to her husband Abram as a wife.

He went in to Hagar, and she conceived; and when she saw that she had conceived, she looked with contempt on her mistress. Then Sarai said to Abram, "May the wrong done to me be on you! I gave my slave-girl to your embrace, and when she saw that she had conceived, she looked on me with contempt. May the Lord judge between you and me!" But Abram said to Sarai, "Your slave-girl is in your power; do to her as you please." Then Sarai dealt harshly with her, and she ran away from her.

The angel of the Lord found her by a spring of water in the wilderness, the spring on the way to Shur. And he said, "Hagar, slave-girl of Sarai, where have you come from and where are you going?" She said, "I am running away from my mistress Sarai." The angel of the Lord said to her, "Return to your mistress, and submit to her."

The angel of the Lord also said to her, "I will so greatly multiply your offspring that they cannot be counted for multi-

tude." And the angel of the Lord said to her, "Now you have conceived and shall bear a son; you shall call him Ishmael, for the Lord has given heed to your affliction. He shall be a wild ass of a man, with his hand against everyone, and everyone's hand against him; and he shall live at odds with all his kin." So she named the Lord who spoke to her, "You are El-roi"; for she said, "Have I really seen God and remained alive after seeing him?" Therefore the well was called Beer-lahai-roi; it lies between Kadesh and Bered.

Hagar bore Abram a son; and Abram named his son, whom Hagar bore, Ishmael. Abram was eighty-six years old when Hagar bore him Ishmael.

Chapter 1

Endure: Hagar

On April 25, 2015 an earthquake ravaged the country of Nepal. It was the worst natural disaster the region had seen in more than eighty years. In some areas, avalanches wiped out entire villages. More than nine thousand people lost their lives, and hundreds of thousands more lost their homes, jobs, and the country as they knew it.

Amidst the media coverage of the disaster were heart-warming photos of newborn babies being rescued from the quake's destruction. My daughter was six months old at the time, and I couldn't help but imagine her as one of those helpless babies buried in rubble, gasping for air and screaming for milk until finally her precious, dust-covered body was lifted up into the safety of loving, safe arms. *A miracle.*

While writing about the earthquake's impact on young mothers and babies, I discovered that there was more to these rescue stories than I initially realized. Many of these babies were born to women employed as surrogates, paid to become pregnant and birth children for other families. While some of the women were Nepalese, most of them had traveled to Nepal from nearby countries like India where the practice of compensated surrogacy is illegal. None of them could have anticipated what would happen while they were there.

After the babies were welcomed with open arms by their parents, the families fled back to their home countries. But the women who birthed those babies were left behind. Suddenly those pictures of rescued infants no longer evoked tender feelings for me. I couldn't stop picturing the women left to endure the emotional trauma of the earthquake's destruction, their bodies exhausted and bleeding from childbirth. Had they been examined by a medical professional? Had their torn flesh been repaired skillfully? Did they have anywhere safe to recover? These women had sacrificed their bodies to fulfill other people's dreams of parenting, and they were left to fend for themselves at their most vulnerable moments.

I couldn't bear the cruel injustice of it all. Who were these self-centered, entitled couples with so much economic privilege that they couldn't muster up compassion for the poor women who had rented them their wombs? How had they become so calloused to the plight of poor people that they could run away from the women who had just birthed their children?

One day while driving to pick up my daughter from school, an episode of the Radiolab podcast called "Birthstory" came up on my iPhone. It followed the story of an Israeli couple who had rescued their twin newborn babies during the earthquake in Nepal. Rolling my eyes and regretting my commitment not to touch my phone while steering my car, I begrudgingly listened—and my heart slowly began to soften, my judgment fade. I learned that Israeli law forbids anyone but heterosexual married couples from adopting children or hiring a surrogate. For these two men in the story who desperately wanted to raise a family, foreign surrogacy was the only way that they could become parents.

Stories like these are always more complex than they might appear at first. That goes for the Bible too. There are stories in our sacred texts that we may think we know well, but when we stop to reexamine them and to look at them through different lenses, we may be surprised by what we see.

The story of Hagar, Sarai, and Abram is one of these stories. Like looking at those pictures from the earthquake in Nepal, I vacillate between rage and compassion, between horror and awe. The stories' complexities draw me in over and over again as I see how the abused become abusers themselves. I watch in dismay as the perpetrators receive blessings instead of justice while the victims are left to die, as the perpetrators are awarded places of honor in our churches while the victims are purposefully left out of our Sunday readings.

Revisiting the story of Sarai, Abram, and Hagar challenges the selective memory of our faith that tends to recall only those parts of our shared story that make us proud. I encourage you to notice any unease this causes in you, and to stay with it. Feel it in your bones. Sit with the troubling realities of the story: that rewards and blessings come to those who abuse their power, and that God does not always bring liberation to the oppressed. Let it stir something troubling within you. Let it open a space for something unexpected to emerge from the wreckage.

SARAI and Abram, later and more commonly known as Sarah and Abraham, long for a baby to continue their family line. Their childlessness is frustrating, even embarrassing, for both of them, but it creates a uniquely painful void for Sarai. While Abram is focused on a future longing—a son to inherit his land—Sarai's desire is more immediate. She wants to be a mother.

God promises Abram that his descendants will be as numerous as the stars in the sky (Gen. 13:5), but the covenant is made with him alone and doesn't necessarily include Sarai. Nothing assures her that her infertility will come to an end. Lifelong childlessness is her deepest fear. Bearing a child is about more than satisfying her inner desires; it's also about proving her womanhood and maintaining her worthiness in the eyes of her husband.

Sarai has good reason not to trust her standing with Abram. Some time ago, while they were traveling together in Egypt, Abram feared that Sarai was a personal liability. If the pharaoh discovered that his wife, a beautiful woman, was married to him, what would stop the pharaoh from killing Abram, so that he could take Sarai for himself? With his life potentially at risk, Abram devised a plan. *I'll pretend that my wife is my sister.* He was prepared to offer up his wife as a sexual slave to the pharaoh in order to protect his own life. Abram said to Sarai, "Say you are my sister, so that it may go well with me because of you, and that my life may be spared on your account" (Gen. 12:13). *If you love me, you'll do this for me*, I read between the lines.

When some Egyptian officials discovered Sarai, they captured her and brought her directly to the pharaoh, just as Abram had feared. We don't need a biblical account of what happens between the pharaoh and Sarai to imagine what she suffered at his hands. Meanwhile Abram greatly benefitted from this arrangement, as he was given live-stock and slaves in exchange for his wife/sister. Among his bounty is an Egyptian woman named Hagar. *A body for a body.*

Eventually Sarai is dismissed from the pharaoh's control, and she is free to return to Abram. But she returns as a victim, bought and sold into sexual slavery while her husband enjoys the spoils of her forced labor. If she didn't know the truth before this moment, she knows it now—that in her husband's eyes she is nothing but a piece of property, a body to be offered up for personal gain.

In turn, Sarai treats Hagar the same way: she is not a human being, but merely a solution to Sarai's problem of childlessness. Hagar is a fertile womb that now belongs to her. She will force Hagar to become her surrogate. Sarai says to Abram, "You see that the Lord has prevented me from bearing children; go in to my slave-girl; it may be that I shall obtain children by her" (Gen. 16:2).

Can Sarai not see what she is doing—how she is perpetuating the cycle of physical and sexual abuse that caused her own suffering? It would be tempting for us to villainize her for this inhumane treatment of Hagar. Sarai is acting selfishly and heartlessly. But she also is acting from a place of woundedness. If she cannot produce a child for Abram, what purpose does she serve in his life? What would prevent him from selling her off to some other powerful man if it benefits him? She must feel powerless over her own body and life, and so she directs all of her fear, all of her rage, and all of her resentment towards Hagar, the one person in her life who holds less power than she does.

When Sarai suggests this plan to her husband—that he will rape Hagar until she becomes pregnant—Abram offers no objection. For the first time in the story, Sarai speaks and she is heard. She finally has some influence over the goings-on in her household, and she immediately abuses that power. The abused becomes the abuser, and the cycle of violence continues.

After some unknown period of time, Hagar does become pregnant. The news falls on Sarai in a way she doesn't anticipate. Instead of relief, she feels threatened. Sarai continues to use Hagar as her personal punching bag. The text reads that Sarai deals harshly with her (Gen. 16:6), continuing the abusive patterns that have defined their relationship.

I know that pregnancy envy is real. While I was trying to conceive, I seemed to encounter someone with a swelling baby bump every time I left the house. Their round bellies seemed to mock me, and their presence filled me with jealousy.

When we have long unmet desires, whether they're for a baby or a romantic partner or an opportunity of some kind, it's natural to notice those who appear to have what we most want. But resentment can become poisonous.

Is this pregnancy, the one that Sarai orchestrated herself, the root cause of her anger? I don't think so. I see it as the trigger. Hagar's pregnancy is a painful reminder of her own empty womb, a void that no amount of power, money, or influence can fill.

WHEN I have pointed out the abusive dynamics in

this passage, the responses have been varied. Like me, most people are stunned and confused by them. Those of us who consider the Bible a source of love, hope, and justice have a hard time reconciling the presence of such a story with the God we know as just, loving, and compassionate. Others like to explain this passage as the relic of an ancient culture in which the social structures permitted such behavior and think it ought to have no bearing on or relevance to the world in which we live today.

If only that were true. If only forced marriage, sexual slavery, and compulsory pregnancy were ancient history.

Today human trafficking enslaves more than twenty-one million people worldwide. Trafficking can take different forms, but in every instance the victim is entrapped, controlled, and exploited by the trafficker, usually for monetary gain. Sometimes victims are moved across international borders, but most often they are trafficked within their home countries, even within their own cities and towns and homes.[1] Child labor, domestic servitude, forced work, and sexual slavery are all forms of human trafficking. For the purposes of this discussion, I will focus specifically on the issue of sex trafficking, as it connects with the story of Hagar and Sarai.

Throughout my years of work advocating for gender justice, I have seen the issue of sex trafficking take center stage in public conversations about the rights of women and girls. Media coverage of incidents like the kidnapping of hundreds of school girls by Boko Haram in Nigeria and large-scale advertising efforts to educate the public about

---

1　　　United Nations Office on Drugs and Crime, "Global Report on Trafficking in Persons," February 2009. http://www.unodc.org/documents/Global_Report_on_TIP.pdf.

sex trafficking during the Super Bowl have raised general awareness about both the global and local prevalence of this crime.

Faith-based groups are important partners in the efforts to end human trafficking. Many religious communities have launched their own initiatives to this end. I'm grateful for this robust response from people of faith, and I believe all of us have a role to play in this movement. What concerns me is the way the matter is often framed. The narrative many of these groups use is based in victimization—that women are vulnerable and need to be rescued. We need only note some of the organizations' names to pick up on this: Project Rescue, Rescue Her, International Rescue Committee. These organizations are doing important work. But the way that we *speak* about our work says something about what we *believe* about our work. Viewing women as primarily in need of the church's rescue is central to the long-standing biblical and societal patriarchal narrative that women cannot speak for themselves or create their own paths to freedom.

I'm also concerned by an almost myopic focus on sex trafficking. When we talk about sexual slavery apart from the many other forms of human trafficking, we distance ourselves from our own culpability in upholding industries that rely on forced labor. If our focus is on saving women and girls from brothels "over there," we may never stop to examine the clothing, food, electronics, and other goods we buy that were produced unethically. In my chapter on Ruth and Naomi, I speak specifically about migrant farm workers who grow, harvest, and pack many of the fruits and vegetables that we consume in the United States.

No matter the form it takes, human trafficking requires that we dehumanize another person. Sex trafficking happens in large part because of how we devalue women overall; viewing their bodies as commodities to be bought, sold, and consumed. At the root of all gender-based violence is the sexist belief that women are inherently inferior to and subordinate to men. This distortion of our worth plays out in all aspects of society, beginning with our most intimate relationships.

In the story of Abram and Sarai, we see trafficking happen not only among strangers, but also *between husband and wife*. Abram values his own life more than the health, dignity, and well-being of Sarai. He voluntarily sells her into sexual slavery to protect himself. Today this kind of abuse continues within the family unit through practices like child marriage, in which girls are sold off in exchange for dowries, often to far older men.

Something that struck me in my research on human trafficking is how often women are the ones trafficking other women and girls. In some countries, women make up the majority of traffickers[2] and many of them have been victims of trafficking themselves. We see this cycle of violence playing out in the biblical story too with Sarai being both the abused and the abuser. This is how sexism becomes internalized. When women cannot see their own humanity, they are not able to see the humanity of other women.

ALTHOUGH I'd been a Bible reader in my youth, I had never encountered the story of Hagar in any meaningful way until college when I read the classic woman-

---

2   United Nations Office on Drugs and Crime, "Global Report on Trafficking in Persons," February 2009.

ist[3] theological text *Sisters in the Wilderness* by Delores
Williams for a class on Black liberation theology. Williams connects this biblical story of slavery and survival
with the experiences of African American women who
throughout history have been forced into surrogate roles
to serve white women and their families. As a white
feminist, this text was revelatory. I could no longer assert in good conscience that women could band together
"as women" without acknowledging the intersections of
racism and sexism, and how these and other systems of
oppression (heterosexism, classism, ableism, ageism, etc.)
are inextricably linked.

Williams' re-telling of Hagar's experience centers on
her survival. After enduring brutal violence and abuse
at the hands of Sarai, Hagar risks everything when she
flees into the wilderness, determined to find her way
back home to Egypt. The Bible is full of escape stories,
but this one is significant for several reasons. As Williams
remarks, Hagar is "the first female in the Bible to liberate
herself from oppressive power structures."[4] I would add
that she is also the first *pregnant* woman to do so.

Several years ago when I was re-reading Hagar's story
for a piece I was writing, I was almost two months pregnant with my daughter. For weeks I had been suffering
from what felt like an unrelenting case of the flu: waves
of nausea that would strike often and with no warning,
sometimes from morning to night; a constant state of
fatigue that made standing up nearly impossible; regular episodes of dizziness, breathlessness, and the shakes.

---

3   *Womanism* is a term coined by Alice Walker to describe a form of
feminism that exists at the intersections of gender and race.
4   Delores S. Williams, *Sisters in the Wilderness: The Challenge of
Womanist God-Talk* (Maryknoll, N.Y.: Orbis Books, 2015), 19.

Here I was, struggling to make the journey from the bed downstairs to the couch, while I was reading the story of a pregnant woman who journeys miles and miles through dangerous terrain in search of safety. It didn't cure my nausea, but it certainly put my mild discomfort into perspective.

I realized then that while Sarai may be able to exert some control over what happens to her body, Hagar is the one who possesses true inner power. Nothing ahead of her is certain, but she knows she cannot stay where she is. Hagar steps out in faith, committed to putting everything on the line for freedom. She musters the strength to keep putting one foot in front of the other, knowing each step is bringing her closer to liberation.

Somewhere along her journey, Hagar encounters a divine presence who speaks to her: "Hagar, slave of Sarai, where have you come from, and where are you going?" (Gen. 16:8). For the first time in the text, she is called by name, and the divine invites her to speak for herself. Surely the divine already knows the answers to these questions, but the asking affirms Hagar as a person with a voice worth hearing and a story worth telling. She answers truthfully: she is running away from her mistress's home. Then, in an unexpected turn, the presence delivers this command: "Return to your mistress, and submit to her" (v. 9). *Go back to your abuser.*

This makes my stomach drop. God shows up in the wilderness to thwart Hagar's escape plan and demand that she return to her life of slavery and oppression? Isn't this the part in the story when God is supposed to bring liberation? I'm tempted to make some logic of this. My only guess is that God was sparing her from something more precarious that awaited her in Egypt. But this is only a guess, and explaining away this verse feels trite and dismissive. When my explanations fail, I tend to turn quickly to the next few verses in which Hagar learns that she will survive the experience, and that her child will live. Yes, Hagar has to return, but she is not sent back without hope. Even so, we cannot escape the fact that God tells a woman to return to her abuser. As Williams rightly names, the divine who speaks to Hagar is "no liberator God."[5]

"Return to your mistress, and submit to her" echoes the times I've been told either implicitly or explicitly to submit to those in authority, even if they have mistreated me and have proven themselves unworthy of my trust and loyalty. It resonates with stories I've heard from survivors of domestic violence. When they confided in their pastors about the abuse they were enduring, their (male) religious leaders told them that they should stay in their marriages, consider their contribution to the violence, and try to work out their difficulties. Part of me fears that if we introduce Hagar's story into our church vernacular, some might point to it as another biblical justification for remaining with an abuser.

We will never understand the reason that God tells Hagar to go back to Sarai's home. We need to hold the discomfort of that reality. While we wrestle with this fact, we also should recognize that God does not ask her to return without assuring her survival. She receives her own divine promise: that she will give birth to a son named Ishmael. His life will not be without turmoil, but then again, as the son of a slave, would she expect anything different for him? But this assurance of survival provides the hope

---

5   Williams, *Sisters in the Wilderness*, 21.

Hagar needs to endure. She trusts that no matter what happens, she will give birth to a son who will grow to be a man. In that moment, this is enough.

Hagar does something quite extraordinary in response: she gives God a new name, "El-Roi," the God who sees. Not only is Hagar the first person in the Bible to give God a new name, but she is also the only one to speak it. This is a relational act, not a transactional one. There is great power in this mutual knowingness—God speaks her name, and she speaks God's name.

Despite everything she has endured—being dehumanized, abused, and exploited by all of those around her—Hagar does not allow these oppressive structures and wounded people to define who she is or what she is worth. When God shows up in the wilderness, speaks to her, and calls her by name, she knows that she is valued and loved, and that she will endure. At her very core, she knows that she is in relationship with the One who sees her for who she is: a child of the divine, a woman of sacred worth, and a person with a story to be told.

Genesis 30:1-22; 35:16-21

When Rachel saw that she bore Jacob no children, she envied her sister; and she said to Jacob, "Give me children, or I shall die!" Jacob became very angry with Rachel and said, "Am I in the place of God, who has withheld from you the fruit of the womb?" Then she said, "Here is my maid Bilhah; go in to her, that she may bear upon my knees and that I too may have children through her." So she gave him her maid Bilhah as a wife; and Jacob went in to her. And Bilhah conceived and bore Jacob a son. Then Rachel said, "God has judged me, and has also heard my voice and given me a son"; therefore she named him Dan. Rachel's maid Bilhah conceived again and bore Jacob a second son. Then Rachel said, "With mighty wrestlings I have wrestled with my sister, and have prevailed"; so she named him Naphtali. When Leah saw that she had ceased bearing children, she took her maid Zilpah and gave her to Jacob as a wife. Then Leah's maid Zilpah bore Jacob a son. And Leah said, "Good fortune!" so she named him Gad. Leah's maid Zilpah bore Jacob a second son. And Leah said, "Happy am I! For the women will call me happy"; so she named him Asher.

In the days of wheat harvest Reuben went and found mandrakes in the field, and brought them to his mother Leah. Then Rachel said to Leah, "Please give me some of your son's mandrakes." But she said to her, "Is it a small matter that you have taken away my husband? Would you take away my son's mandrakes also?" Rachel said, "Then he may lie with you tonight for your son's mandrakes." When Jacob came from the field in the evening, Leah went out to meet him, and said, "You must

come in to me; for I have hired you with my son's mandrakes."
So he lay with her that night. And God heeded Leah, and she
conceived and bore Jacob a fifth son. Leah said, "God has given
me my hire because I gave my maid to my husband"; so she
named him Issachar. And Leah conceived again, and she bore
Jacob a sixth son. Then Leah said, "God has endowed me with
a good dowry; now my husband will honor me, because I have
borne him six sons"; so she named him Zebulun. Afterwards
she bore a daughter, and named her Dinah. Then God remembered Rachel, and God heeded her and opened her womb.

Then they journeyed from Bethel; and when they were still
some distance from Ephrath, Rachel was in childbirth, and she
had hard labor. When she was in her hard labor, the midwife
said to her, "Do not be afraid; for now you will have another
son." As her soul was departing (for she died), she named him
Ben-oni; but his father called him Benjamin. So Rachel died,
and she was buried on the way to Ephrath (that is, Bethlehem), and Jacob set up a pillar at her grave; it is the pillar of
Rachel's tomb, which is there to this day.

Israel journeyed on, and pitched his tent beyond the tower of
Eder.

Chapter 2

Remember: Rachel

When we name someone or something, we are purposefully creating meaning in our lives. We name what is precious to us: our children, our pets, and sometimes even possessions like cars. Names signify importance, belonging, and identity.

Naming is evident all over the Bible. In the first chapter of Genesis, God brings creation into being through the language of naming as God calls the light and the waters and all creatures into existence. God gives a new name to mark a significant shift in a person's life: "Sarai" and "Abram" become Sarah and Abraham as a sign of God's covenant with them; "Saul" becomes Paul after his conversion experience. Hagar gives God a new name, *El-Roi*, "the God who sees."

I try hard to remember the names of people I meet. I recently started teaching group exercise classes at my local gym, and I've realized how important remembering someone's name can be in that setting. It establishes trust, familiarity, and a sense of belonging.

Names often have stories behind them. Some people are named after beloved grandparents while others are named after their parents' favorite musicians or artists. Transgender persons often claim new names for themselves that better reflect who they are.

I come from a line of Kathryns, a name I received from my beloved maternal grandmother "Honey." I've continued the lineage, passing it down to my daughter as her middle name. Her first name, Samantha, was chosen months before I became pregnant at a time when my husband and I honestly weren't completely sold on the idea of parenthood. But, since we were considering the possibility and we love to plan things way in advance, the topic of baby names came up one day in casual conversation. "I love the name Samantha for a girl," Matt said. *Samantha— yes!*

When I was nine years old, I fell in love with a doll named Samantha, one of the original dolls from the *American Girl* line. At that age I hadn't been all that interested in dolls, but Samantha was different somehow. With dark hair and eyes and a pale complexion, she resembled me a little. One evening I managed to sneak the *American Girl* catalogue up to my bedroom, and night after night, I examined the pages of it, admiring the dolls adorned in exquisite clothing with perfectly matching accessories. I wanted one so badly.

Even though Christmas was coming, I was old enough to know that it was impractical to hope for a doll like that. Samantha was costly, and by that age I knew, much to my mother's chagrin, that gifts under the tree came for her, not from Santa Claus. My parents had separated earlier that year, and money was even tighter than usual. Not wanting to make anyone feel guilty on Christmas morning, I opted to write "paper dolls" on my wish list that year.

That Christmas morning when it was time for me to open a gift, I began to peel back the carefully wrapped paper of a large box and found myself in disbelief as the familiar American Girl logo emerged from under the red and white foil. Slowly lifting the large white lid of the gift box, I was in awe of the doll held inside. She was even more exquisite than I could've imagined. *And she was mine.*

Later I would learn the story of how my Samantha doll ended up under the tree. My grandmother was months from death, and she knew this would be her last Christmas. She told my mother that she wanted to buy me the doll plus all the bells and whistles that came with it. Honestly, I think the doll was as much for the two of them as it was for me. After the packages arrived, my grandmother and mother opened up all the boxes, taking out each and every tiny piece to admire. My Samantha doll is the only toy from my childhood that I still have, a connection to the generations of women in my family who have loved me and sacrificed for me to experience a life of fullness and joy.

If I ever had a daughter, it seemed only fitting that I would give her the name Samantha. My grandmother would have loved that. I wish she had lived long enough to meet our daughter, but I hope that by my act of naming her I've helped to keep Honey's love and memory alive.

When the story of Rachel ends, she is on her deathbed after giving birth to her second son. Her life is cut tragically short, and she knows that her son will have no memory of her. With her last breath, she ends her life with a final act of naming: she gives her son a name that will memorialize her struggle to bring new life into the world—a life she will never know.

UNLIKE other stories in the Bible, the writer of Rachel's story is careful to name all of the actors involved. We know from reading other biblical stories that if women are mentioned, they are often unnamed or solely identified by their male relatives or offspring. *So-and-so's wife. So-and-so's mother.* This story is an exception, though it's probably less about affirming women as people and more about avoiding confusion. After all there are four different women who become sexually involved with Jacob.

There is Rachel (Hebrew for "ewe"), the daughter of Laban and the younger sister of Leah, who is usually only remembered for—what else?—her physical appearance. While out tending her family's flocks of sheep, Rachel catches the attention of a stranger named Jacob (Hebrew for "supplanter"). Jacob is so taken with her beauty that without so much as an introduction he approaches her, kisses her, and begins to cry with joy before revealing that he is her cousin: Laban is his uncle. He certainly knows how to make an impression. Rachel goes home to share with her family the details of this bizarre encounter with an unfamiliar cousin.

At Laban's invitation, Jacob comes to stay with his family. We can only imagine what Rachel's thoughts on this arrangement are. Jacob is delighted; he is smitten with Rachel and has no qualms revealing just how much he desires to be with her. He offers Laban seven years of labor if he will agree to let Jacob marry her. Finally, after those long, laborious years have passed, the time comes for Jacob and Rachel to wed. But Laban has other plans. On the wedding night, Laban sends his elder daughter Leah to the marriage bed intended for her sister. In the dark, both figuratively and literally, Jacob is completely unaware of the bridal switch that Laban has orchestrated, and consummates his marriage not with Rachel but with Leah instead.

When we studied this text in my seminary Hebrew Bible class, the term my professor used to describe Laban's action was "trickery." He reminded us that Jacob has also been a trickster, taking for himself the blessing that his father had intended for his brother Esau. On a literary level, I understand this parallelism in the story, but as an advocate for gender justice, I find the term "trickery" woefully inadequate to describe the depth of betrayal and immorality in Laban's actions toward his two daughters and Jacob. He exploits his nephew and treats his daughters as nothing more than interchangeable pieces in a game for power and control.

When Jacob confronts his father-in-law, Laban cites cultural norms as his rationale for what he has done: "This is not done in our country—giving the younger [daughter] before the firstborn" (Gen. 29:26). Perhaps this would have been a legitimate concern had Laban expressed it the moment Jacob shared his desire to marry Rachel seven years ago. Instead Laban allowed his nephew to labor for seven years, all the while plotting against him. *I want another seven years, Jacob.*

In the end, Jacob begrudgingly agrees to additional years of labor under Laban's roof, and he marries Rachel the very week after sharing his marriage bed with Leah. That's two marriages in one week, two sisters with the same husband, all of them living together under their father's roof. A dysfunctional family indeed.

Leah and Rachel are more than sisters now; they are wives pitted against one another for their husband's affection. The text reads that when God sees that Leah is unloved (Leah actually says that she is hated by Jacob), God opens her womb to conceive (Gen. 29:31). Leah gives birth to Jacob's first son Reuben, and then his second son Simeon. Rachel, struggling to get pregnant, remains childless. Consumed with frustration and grief over her infertility, Rachel cries out to Jacob, "Give me children, or I shall die!" (Gen. 30:1). In her place and time, *a barren woman might as well have been dead.* Women were defined solely by their ability to bear children. As Rachel observes her sister conceive, give birth, and conceive again with such apparent ease, Rachel understandably grows concerned about her future and resentful of her sister's fertility.

Really, the one Rachel should be raging against is God. Even Jacob hints at this in his emotional response to Rachel's demand: "Am I in the place of God, who has withheld from you the fruit of the womb?" (Gen. 30:2). Has God actively intervened to prevent Rachel from conceiving? Has God closed Rachel's womb? Hebrew Bible scholar Joel Baden notes that there is a subtle yet important distinction for us to consider. He argues that we should not equate Leah's divine *blessing* of fertility with a subsequent divine *curse* of infertility for Rachel.[1]

---

1   Joel S. Baden, "The Nature of Barrenness in the Hebrew Bible," *Disability Studies and Biblical Literature* (2011): 13–27.

Both women start from the same "natural" state — not yet having conceived — and God intercedes on Leah's behalf to open her womb.

Perhaps a lack of positive divine intervention for Rachel technically ought not to be equated with a curse. Even so, I imagine that this perceived inaction on God's part leaves Rachel feeling cursed even if she is not actually cursed. Remember her words to Jacob: *give me children or I shall die.*

We've already seen how this kind of desperation can manifest itself. Rachel, like Sarai, sees only one option available and resorts to forcing one of her handmaidens to marry Jacob, so that she may bear children on her mistress's behalf. Bilhah becomes Rachel's surrogate and births two sons conceived with Jacob. And like Sarai's experience, these baby boys do not bring Rachel the maternal satisfaction she hoped they would. In naming them Dan (meaning "judgment") and Naphtali (meaning "my struggle") she makes it clear that her desires remain painfully unmet.

The births of Dan and Naphtali do little to assuage Rachel's lingering self-doubt about her importance in Jacob's life, and they only exacerbate the tensions with her sister. With two new sons in the family, Leah has lost her upper hand as the sole wife who bears children and ensures Jacob's lineage. Not to be outdone by her younger sister, Leah proceeds to gives her handmaid Zilpah to Jacob as a wife, and she also births two sons. [2] Two enslaved women give birth to four baby boys, all in an effort to overcome

---

2   I do not want to ignore the forced marriage and surrogacy of Rachel and Leah's slaves. But since this was such a focus of my chapter on Hagar, I will not repeat what I have said there on this topic.

the marital strife shared by two insecure sisters.

Unlike Hagar, who speaks for herself in the text, Bilhah and Zilpah are completely silenced in this story. We know them only as handmaidens, second-class wives of Jacob, and forced surrogates for their wealthy, privileged mistresses. They are by far the most marginalized characters in this story. They remind us again of how the oppressed easily become the oppressors. Though Rachel and Leah are affected by patriarchal practices, they are also women of means with access to power that they then wield over women like Bilhah and Zilpah.

DESPITE her sins against Bilhah, Rachel does obtain the desires of her heart. After all she has done and all of the people she has harmed in her quest for a child, Rachel conceives and gives birth to a son whom she names Joseph (meaning "he adds"). The moment she lays eyes on her newborn baby, she exclaims, "May God add to me another son!" Mere seconds after the exhausting and depleting experience of childbirth, Rachel knows this one baby is not enough. She wants more. Again, her prayers are answered and she becomes pregnant a second time.

At the time of Rachel's second pregnancy, Jacob and his brood of wives, slaves, and children are journeying from Bethel back to their home in Ephrath. After fourteen years of servitude, Jacob finally is free of Laban's grip on his life. Before they make it to Ephrath, Rachel goes into labor. The strain of travel may have induced contractions prematurely, and her labor is difficult. Something is not right, and Rachel knows it. As the hours pass, she grows weaker. *This is not like it was when I gave birth to Joseph.* She is not going to survive this.

Rachel's longing for children defines many years of her life, and when she finally has what she wants, it is taken from her. In giving life she loses her own. Does she remember the words she cried out to Jacob years earlier, "Give me children, or I shall die?" Does she remember at the birth of Joseph asking God for another child? Does she regret that prayer?

In the pauses between painful contractions, I wonder whether she is thinking about the child she will never know—and who will never know her—and for her young son Joseph who will barely remember her. Each contraction elicits the groans of a woman not only in excruciating physical pain, but who is experiencing soul-crushing grief over what will never be.

The midwife attending the birth recognizes that this is not a normal labor, and that Rachel is in distress. If the labor continues much longer, she knows that both mother and baby will die. She does what she can to ease Rachel's pain, coaxing her into different positions, bringing water for her to sip, speaking gently and firmly for her to focus. *Each contraction brings you closer to meeting your baby.* "Do not be afraid," the midwife reassures her.

WHEN I was pregnant with my daughter, I suddenly found myself the target of what I refer to as "birth war stories." Women who were complete strangers would accost with the most horrifying details about their labors and deliveries. "I had to get an emergency C-section or I would've died!" "I was in labor for forty-eight hours and still hadn't made any progress." As an advocate for improving maternal health, I knew what could go wrong during childbirth, so I was already fearful. Being on the receiving end of these horrifying tales only increased my worries. At the advice of my midwife, I began surrounding myself with positive birth narratives from books like Ina May's *Guide to Childbirth*. Each of them revealed something new and different about the experience, and I discovered there was a moment they all shared: at some point each woman felt as if she could endure no more and began to doubt herself.

That was true of my own birth experience. I had been laboring in the birthing tub for hours when my midwife encouraged me to shift into a new position. As I moved from laying on my back into a deep squat, the next contraction was so powerful that my water broke. The intense sensation of that nearly sent me into a state of panic. I lost my sense of center, and in response to the fear I was experiencing, my whole body began to seize up, ready to flee the scene. I didn't know how to regain control of my breathing. I felt as if I was drowning in pain.

When the contraction finally passed, I began to sob, exhausted, overwhelmed, and fearful of what was to come. *I can't do this anymore.* I looked to my midwife with pleading eyes. *Help me.* She took my hand and firmly but kindly reassured me, "You are ok. Everything is ok. I know you afraid, but you can do this." From that moment forward I never lost my focus again.

"Do not be afraid," the midwife says to Rachel, sensing that the end is near for both the birth and for her life. As she looks into the laboring woman's eyes, she must recognize that familiar look of all-consuming fear. Unlike the midwife who coached me to hold fast to my inner strength, Rachel's midwife cannot in good faith offer words of reassurance. She knows Rachel is not going to survive this. She needs to find some way to keep Rachel going long enough to deliver her baby safely. She speaks the few words of hopeful promise she can muster: "Do not be afraid, for you will have another son." And with that remaining bit of strength Rachel pushes her second precious child into the world. As her slippery, pink newborn takes his first breath, Rachel breathes her last, speaking one final word: *Ben-Oni.* "Son of my sorrows."

Surely this is not the name she has planned to give her son. Nothing is as she had hoped it would be. There is so much left unsaid. There are so many things she wants to share with her little boy, the one for whom she has wept and prayed all of these years. Now he is here, and she is gone.

RACHEL'S death might strike us as tragic, but perhaps not all that surprising. We may have an easier time accepting that a woman in those days would have lost her life during childbirth since she didn't have access to the medical technology we do today. No one really knew how to keep women alive during and after a difficult labor and delivery. This is not to discount the work of midwives who certainly had their own strategies for helping laboring women in distress, but their resources were understandably limited. Considering all of the medical advances that have been made in maternal and child health over the last century, shouldn't maternal death be an anomaly these days?

The statistics tell a startling different story. Complications from childbirth are the number one cause of death for women of childbearing age in the developing world. Nearly eight hundred women die daily from complications during pregnancy or childbirth or within the first month after giving birth. More than 250,000 women each year lose their lives while trying to bring new life into the world, leaving behind children, families, and communities. Tragically, women often die from easily preventable or treatable causes like infection and hemorrhaging; others die from complications from unsafe abortion in countries where the procedure is illegal and desperate women are forced to seek care from disreputable sources.

I often refer to this high rate of maternal mortality as a moral tragedy because saving women's lives in childbirth does not depend on us discovering a cure. We already know what we need to do to prevent many of these deaths. But we have not done all that we can to ensure that every single woman, no matter where she lives, has access to the basic care she needs to ensure her well-being in labor. We may not be able to stop every single maternal death from happening, but there's a lot more we can do to make childbirth safer for everyone.

What makes all of this even more tragic to me is the fact that some women are dying from pregnancies that they would have prevented had they had access to reliable forms of contraception. Women know that their bodies have limits. Pregnancy is grueling on the body, especially if a woman has recently given birth. Ensuring access to family planning will not bring an end to maternal mortality, but it's an important component of reducing it. In fact, global health experts estimate that if every woman who wanted family planning had access to it, maternal deaths would drop by a third.

Family planning doesn't only prevent the deaths of women in childbirth. It's a critical, life-affirming tool that enables women and couples to determine the timing, spacing, and (ideally) the number of children they want. The creation of our families, whatever they may look like, is sacred work, and every person deserves to have all of the information and resources needed to do so thoughtfully, prayerfully, and intentionally.

OFTENTIMES in our discussions about health disparities like these, particularly when the burden lands on those living in poverty, I find that folks who possess a certain economic privilege tend to become fixated on addressing short-term suffering. I understand that impulse. In a genuine effort to be helpful, we want to do something in the moment. We want an easy, immediate solution that we can execute right now.

I'm not immune to this way of thinking. Early on in my advocacy work for maternal health, I made a strategic mistake along these lines. I wanted to give churches some ideas for what they could do to help end maternal mortality, so I presented a very tactile project that a colleague had shared with me: the healthy birthing kit. It was a basic set of supplies—a sheet of plastic, a razor blade, soap, string, and gloves—that anyone could put together and send to our relief agency for distribution. When administered properly, the birthing kit could double a birthing woman's chance of survival in childbirth by reducing the risk of infection. Easy. Simple. Effective.

As soon as I mentioned the kits, the rest of my presentation was a wash. All the questions I received were about how to make the kits. I'd meant to mention the kits in passing, not make it the focus of my entire talk. I was happy to see people engaged and excited to do something, but they were so fixated on helping that they didn't stop to wonder what it meant for there to be a need for the kits in the first place. The birthing kit project took off and before I knew it, I got a frantic call from our relief agency. The person who handled the kits pleaded with me to discourage folks from sending them any more birthing kits. Their supply was full, and they'd run out of space to store them.

I learned a hard lesson from that experience, and when the birthing kits came up in later conversations, I asked folks some challenging questions: What did it mean that churches in the United States had to put together sheets of plastic and bars of soap and ship them halfway around the world so that a woman could have a healthy birth? Kits weren't going to end maternal mortality. The healthy birth kit was a short-term bandage, not a long-term solution.

Some people might argue that exporting practices, like contraceptives, that have been developed by Western medicine, is another bandage—or worse yet, a tool of white supremacy. Many have rightly criticized past practices of global population control that intended to limit the population growth of poorer countries. Right here in the United States, Black women were forcibly sterilized for decades to limit their family size while indigenous children were taken from their parents to be raised "properly" by white Christian families. Reproductive coercion in any form is abhorrent and sinful. No one should be forced into any decision regarding their bodies, health, or families.

In a similar vein we should consider how the pressure to have a child—in some places, many children—can negatively affect a woman's health. I remember a doctor from India telling me the story of a husband who brought his wife in for treatment. What the husband wanted was for the doctor to give his wife some medicine that would increase her energy. She was tired all of the time. The woman said nothing, but the doctor knew what was happening. She said to the husband, "Your wife is tired from having so many children. She needs a break from pregnancy." After giving birth to child after child, her body was depleted. Not one to mince words, the doctor told the man bluntly, "If your wife gets pregnant again, she will die." The man retorted, "Then I will get another wife."

EVEN in the best of circumstances when a pregnancy is planned and wanted, things can go wrong. Even when all the interventions are accessible and available, tragedy cannot always be prevented. Terrible things still happen. If Rachel were to give birth today, who knows whether things would turn out any differently in the end.

After Rachel dies, Jacob gives his newborn son a new name: Benjamin. He cannot bear to call his baby boy "Son of my Sorrow." But there is no name change that will erase the mark of a mother gone too soon. Rachel will not be replaced. And we will make sure that she is never forgotten.

Exodus 1:8-2:10

Now a new king arose over Egypt, who did not know Joseph. He said to his people, "Look, the Israelite people are more numerous and more powerful than we. Come, let us deal shrewdly with them, or they will increase and, in the event of war, join our enemies and fight against us and escape from the land." Therefore they set taskmasters over them to oppress them with forced labor. They built supply cities, Pithom and Rameses, for Pharaoh. But the more they were oppressed, the more they multiplied and spread, so that the Egyptians came to dread the Israelites. The Egyptians became ruthless in imposing tasks on the Israelites, and made their lives bitter with hard service in mortar and brick and in every kind of field labor. They were ruthless in all the tasks that they imposed on them.

The king of Egypt said to the Hebrew midwives, one of whom was named Shiphrah and the other Puah, "When you act as midwives to the Hebrew women, and see them on the birthstool, if it is a boy, kill him; but if it is a girl, she shall live." But the midwives feared God; they did not do as the king of Egypt commanded them, but they let the boys live. So the king of Egypt summoned the midwives and said to them, "Why have you done this, and allowed the boys to live?" The midwives said to Pharaoh, "Because the Hebrew women are not like the Egyptian women; for they are vigorous and give birth before the midwife comes to them." So God dealt well with the midwives; and the people multiplied and became very strong. And because the midwives feared God, he gave them families. Then Pharaoh commanded all

*his people, "Every boy that is born to the Hebrews you shall
throw into the Nile, but you shall let every girl live."
Now a man from the house of Levi went and married a
Levite woman. The woman conceived and bore a son; and
when she saw that he was a fine baby, she hid him three
months. When she could hide him no longer she got a papyrus basket for him, and plastered it with bitumen and pitch;
she put the child in it and placed it among the reeds on the
bank of the river. His sister stood at a distance, to see what
would happen to him.*

*The daughter of Pharaoh came down to bathe at the river,
while her attendants walked beside the river. She saw the
basket among the reeds and sent her maid to bring it. When
she opened it, she saw the child. He was crying, and she took
pity on him, "This must be one of the Hebrews' children,"
she said. Then his sister said to Pharaoh's daughter, "Shall
I go and get you a nurse from the Hebrew women to nurse
the child for you?" Pharaoh's daughter said to her, "Yes."
So the girl went and called the child's mother. Pharaoh's
daughter said to her, "Take this child and nurse it for me,
and I will give you your wages." So the woman took the
child and nursed it. When the child grew up, she brought
him to Pharaoh's daughter, and she took him as her son. She
named him Moses, "because," she said, "I drew him out of
the water."*

Chapter 3

Resist: The Exodus Midwives and Mothers

As part of my maternal health advocacy initiative, I had the opportunity to connect with global health workers from around the world who are doing the hard, day-to-day work of keeping women and their babies alive and healthy.

One fall I spent several weeks traveling around with Alice Otieno, a community health nurse who runs a small health facility on the banks of Lake Victoria in a rural part of Kenya called Kopagana. I brought Alice to the United States to speak to some of our congregations about her work.

Years ago, Alice felt a call to provide medical care to the people of Kopanga, a population of more than ten thousand whom she calls "the forgotten people." With sky-high numbers of new HIV infections, alarming rates of maternal and infant mortality, and abject poverty, the people who live in Kopanga are among the most disenfranchised populations of our world.

Alice started her medical ministry in a small room in a house, paying the rent out of her own pocket. Local churchwomen who believed in her mission donated supplies. Through her work, her health facility has since grown into a nine-room clinic staffed by three nurses who see at least a thousand patients every month. Those seeking medical care often travel long distances on foot in order to get their babies vaccinated, to get tested for HIV, or to obtain contraceptives.

When I met Alice in 2010, the clinic had no running water or reliable electricity, and they often ran out of critical supplies. Despite these daily challenges and frustrations, Alice had been able to achieve the near impossible: eradicating measles in the community by making sure each and every child born in the area was vaccinated. This amazed me. "How in the world were you able to do that?" I asked her.

Alice shared that one day not long after she had opened her clinic, a young mother came in with her infant child who was ill with bronchitis. She couldn't get the coughing to stop. Though Alice didn't have much on hand, she had exactly what she needed to help. Alice draped a clean bed sheet over the woman and her baby like a tent. She then carefully placed inside that tent a pot of boiling water filled with menthol crystals to create a healing steam that would loosen the baby's cough. After some time the baby's lungs cleared, and her coughing subsided. The woman was so grateful that she went back to her village and told everyone the story of how Alice had made her baby well. Sounds a lot like Jesus to me.

"I have cared for my community for many years," Alice told me. "I have shown them that I love them by showing up every day at the clinic. I treat them with kindness. Now they trust me to take care of them and their children." That's the secret of her success.

During our travels together, Alice and I discussed the importance of family planning counseling as a critical health intervention for the women who come to her clinic. Her greatest challenge was not that women rejected contraception; her problem was that she couldn't get enough contraceptives to keep on hand. Even though the Kenyan government provided her with quarterly supplies of contraceptive injections—the preferred method for most of the women—the demand was so high that the hundred vials they received every three months lasted only three weeks. At the time a single dose of the injection cost about $2.00, but for women living in poverty, that's more than a day's pay. Sadly, Alice told me that she and her staff have to turn many women away empty-handed, recommending that they return in a few months when their supply has been replenished. All they can do is pray that the women don't get pregnant in the meantime.

"Why are contraceptive injections in such high demand among the women in your community?" I asked her. Alice does have other methods of contraception on hand, including birth control pills and condoms, but few people ask for them. Pills are hard to keep track of. Condoms aren't appealing to men. Even if women insist their partners use them, men often refuse. A contraceptive injection is appealing because it's highly effective, long lasting, and undetectable. Alice explained that many men in Kenya do not support their wives in delaying or preventing a pregnancy because they define their masculinity by the number of children they have fathered. No matter the cost to their partners' health or to their other children's overall well-being, men want large families, so that they can feel like "real men."

These birth control injections allow women to be sur-reptitious in their pregnancy prevention. The male part-ner, whether he approves of contraceptive use or not, has no ability to control her fertility. Ideally, partners would be in agreement about plans for their families, but when an ill-timed pregnancy could pose a serious threat to a woman's health or otherwise jeopardize her well-being, she must find a way to save her own life.

Alice shared with me an unsettling incident that hap-pened when the irate husband of a patient confronted her at the clinic. He angrily demanded that Alice confess to helping his wife obtain contraceptives without his con-sent. "It's your fault that my wife isn't getting pregnant!" he screamed at her. Alice remained calm. She would not be intimidated or bullied into divulging confidential information about one of her patients. Neither confirming nor denying the allegation, she simply told him, "If you and your wife want another child, I would advise you to keep trying."

Throughout our time together, I noted all of the dif-ferent ways that Alice exhibited courage: starting a clinic with little funding, working in an area far from her hus-band and two daughters, providing life-saving services to people who otherwise would have no care, and standing up to the men who try to control the health and well-be-ing of the women she is committed to serve.

Alice reminds me of the clever and brave Hebrew midwives Shiphrah and Puah who were instrumental in saving the lives of countless Hebrew baby boys, including Moses. Their creative thinking and swift action protected helpless baby boys from the threat of violence. Much like Alice today, they faithfully answered the call to care for the most vulnerable, no matter the cost.

If your faith community follows the lectionary, the names Shiprah and Puah may be familiar to you because you've probably heard their story read from the pulpit. Unlike many other biblical texts involving women that have been omitted, the passage in which their story is found is included in the Revised Standard Lectionary, which assigns Scripture readings for weekly worship in a three-year rotation.

The editorial decision to include or exclude a certain passage is not a neutral one. Truly, as Marjorie Procter-Smith noted of the entire lectionary process, when we read our texts aloud in worship, we re-tell a story of who we are. In its current form, the lectionary cannot include every single verse. Those who hold the decision-making power of the lectionary's structure divide the passages they deem "essential" to the Christian story from those they do not. Interestingly, the occasional story involving a woman rarely fits neatly into this narrative arc. The story of Shiprah and Puah is an exception. As Procter-Smith notes, the content of the biblical stories already over-whelmingly centers and privileges the experience of men. When we leave biblical stories of women out of our shared readings, we only reinforce an identity that is male-centered.[1] Thankfully the existence of narratives like that of Shiprah and Puah reveals a different reality.

---

1   Marjorie Procter-Smith, "Beyond the New Lectionary: A Constructive Critique," *Quarterly Review* 13 (Summer 1993): 49–58.

THE STORY of Shiphrah and Puah begins by describing a time when the Egyptian pharaoh has forced the Hebrew people into slavery. Though they are enslaved and oppressed, they greatly outnumber the Egyptian people, and the king worries that soon they will have the power to rise up and defeat his regime. He begins plotting ways to stifle the growth of the Hebrew people. He tasks them with the hard labor of building new cites. But no matter how hard they work, the Hebrew people continue to grow in number. Sensing an increasing threat to his reign, the pharaoh resorts to violence. He orders Shiphrah and Puah to slaughter every newborn Hebrew boy.

Why does the king specify that only baby boys should be killed? Why spare the baby girls? As bearers of the Hebrew lineage, male children ensure the longevity of their people. If the pharaoh can wipe out the boys, the Hebrew girls will grow up without potential partners among their people. Eventually they will marry and have children with Egyptian men. Without boys, Hebrew girls pose no threat to the Egyptian regime. In fact, they are assets as future slaves, concubines, and wives who will bear Egyptian children and thus solidify the pharaoh's power.

The major flaw of the pharaoh's plan is that he relies on the midwives' cooperation. He wrongly assumes that Hebrew boys pose the real threat to his power. As Jewish scholar Inbar Raveh notes, women in this story are far more dangerous than the men. She writes, "Instead of being a tool in the king's hands and killing the Hebrew infants at birth, [the midwives] mount a powerful resistance against the repressive and authoritarian forces symbolized by the regime."[2] Their story is a perfect example of how women use the knowledge, access, and resources they have to find ways to push back against terror, violence, and injustice.

What the king fails to recognize is that Shiphrah and Puah fear God more than they fear him, and they refuse to comply. After some time, when he realizes they have failed to follow his orders, he brings them in for questioning and demands an explanation for their lack of obedience. "Why have you done this and allowed the boys to lives?" (Ex. 1:18) I venture that when Shiphrah and Puah make a conscious decision to resist the king, they know a confrontation like this is inevitable. So, in advance they put their heads together and devised a clever plan for how they will respond when the time comes. *We will tell the king that the Hebrew women have babies so quickly that we are never able to make it to the birth in time.*

Isn't this brilliant? What is so savvy about their evasion of the truth is that they know the king has limits to his power: he has no access to the birthing room. He has no knowledge or experience of women giving birth. Unless he personally plans to infiltrate the birthing spaces of Hebrew women, the king has no definitive proof that they are lying. As they are the exclusive holders of all birth knowledge, Shiphrah and Puah strategically dismiss the king's accusations, which spares their lives for now, and extends their hedge of protection over the Hebrew people.

Besides, even if Shiphrah and Puah are sufficiently intimidated by his power to obey his command and to commit acts of infanticide, undoubtedly word of this violence

2   Inbar Raveh, "'They let the children live': the midwives at a political crossroads." Nashim: A Journal of Jewish Women's Studies and Gender Issues 24 (2013): 11+. General OneFile. Web. Last accessed 12 April, 2016.

will spread quickly throughout the Hebrew community. If Shiphrah and Puah do not resist the oppressive powers of the king, the Hebrew women surely will. Pregnant women will find a way to prevent the midwives from entering the birthing spaces in order to protect their children.

Even with their cleverness, the midwives are not safe from danger. If the king has no qualms about calling for the death of newborn babies, he would have no problem killing them right then and there. Although they leave unharmed, we ought to remember that they are willing to face the severe if not lethal consequences of remaining faithful to their sacred calling.

There's a reason Shiphrah and Puah are the only people named in the first chapter of Exodus: they are the real protagonists in this story of survival and resistance to state-ordered infanticide. Together they demonstrate immense courage in the face of imminent violence, and their courage paves the way for the birth of Moses and the eventual exodus of the Hebrew people.

MIDWIVES have been the sacred keepers of childbirth throughout history. But due to the medicalization (and white masculinization) of childbirth through modern medical practices, we may be unfamiliar with the care they provide, or we may even consider their expertise less than that of obstetricians. As my friend and author Rachel Marie Stone has said, "We [in the United States] tend to have a strong faith in the possibility and power and preferability of a medical approach to birth—'with a doctor, in a hospital, is best.'"[3]

---

3   Rachel Marie Stone, "Engaging Mothers Globally, Knowing Our History," 2012 presentation.

This preference for a hospital birth attended by an obstetrician, however, is not universal; it's cultural. In many other parts of the world, midwives are highly regarded as trusted providers of medical care for pregnant and laboring women. One could argue that this is in part due to the fact that in many rural areas hospitals and doctors are not available. This is true, and while medical interventions are critical when a laboring woman encounters complications, they are not always necessary otherwise.

The World Health Organization has stated that midwives who receive adequate training are well suited to provide eighty-seven percent of the care that birthing women and their newborn babies need.[4] It's no wonder that increasing the number of trained midwives, particularly in countries without robust health infrastructures, is considered a "best buy" for increasing access to primary care and for lowering rates of maternal and infant mortality.

Since I was fortunate to have a healthy, complication-free pregnancy, I turned to midwives for my prenatal care and for attending my birth. Before my pregnancy, I'd never considered using a midwife for my health care, but at the recommendation of a friend I watched the documentary *The Business of Being Born*, produced by Rickie Lake, that strongly advocates for midwife-attended homebirth as a viable, safe option for women living in the United States. Like any documentary, *The Business of Being Born* has its point of view and its limitations, but it motivated me to research what all of my birthing options were. Ultimately, I decided to work with an independent birthing center that felt more like a home than a medical

---

4   United Nations Population Fund, The State of the World's Midwifery, 2014. http://www.unfpa.org/sowmy.

facility.

The care and attention I received from the midwife team was unlike any I'd received from other medical providers in the past. Their whole approach to prenatal visits was woman-focused, holistic, and personal. I didn't feel like a patient there; I felt like a person. I giggled when we pulled into the parking lot of the practice for the first time and saw a few cars sporting bumper stickers that read, "Midwives help people out."

My decision to opt for a birth outside of a hospital elicited a lot of strong opinions from friends and strangers alike. Most women who'd had hospital births were either horrified that I'd willingly turn down access to pain medication or amused that I thought I could handle labor without any interventions. In the end I was fortunate to have the birth that I had hoped and planned for, which I know is not always the case. When complications arise, our plans often go by the wayside out of necessity. I give thanks for my complication-free birth, facilitated by compassionate midwives, nurses, a doula, and my husband who journeyed alongside me through the ordeal.

Preparing to deliver at a birth center required some new ways of thinking about childbirth. In the past I had assumed that I would give birth in a hospital, lying on my back, with an epidural administered to relieve the pain of contractions—just like I'd seen in movies. I say this not to disregard or diminish any woman who chooses or needs to birth this way, but more to point out that I had never known that any other option was available to me. Frankly I was clueless about birth. Even though I'd been advocating for maternal health for years, I'd never actually seen a birth in real life. All I had to go on were depictions in popular culture that followed the same general storyline: woman's water breaks in grocery store. Awestruck partner panics and drives maniacally to the hospital. Woman yells obscenities. Male doctor screams at her to push. Baby is born. Afterwards, mom's tummy is suddenly flat, and her hair looks like she just returned from the salon.

This fictionalized birth story is problematic. When we sanitize and sensationalize birth, we minimize its power. When we romanticize birth, we minimize its danger. The process of bringing new life into this world has never been something a woman does without risk to her health and life. There are ordinary moments when I'm in the middle of a group of strangers and I think to myself, "It truly is a miracle that we are all here."

During my year of working with midwives, I found that they shared that same sense of awe I had. Their work is sacred; they accompany women during some of their most vulnerable moments and their most powerful life experiences. Having received this kind of support and care, I appreciate even more deeply the story of Shiphrah and Puah and their refusal to desecrate the everyday, ordinary miracles that take place in the birthing room.

THE midwives' resistance paves the way for the birth of Moses. Like other infancy narratives found in the Bible, the text tells us next to nothing about how this baby entered the world. The story jumps from conception to birth in half a verse. But we can imagine the tumultuous nine months that Moses's mother endures as she anticipates the birth of her child. The pharaoh has given up on the midwives slaughtering boys in the birth room and moves on to Plan B: throw all of the baby boys into the Nile River to drown.

I wonder, given the circumstances of the times, whether Moses's mother hopes for a girl instead of a boy? A baby girl will be left unharmed, but if the pharaoh's army discovers that her baby is a boy, he will be killed.

Moses's father is mentioned briefly and then is noticeably absent for the rest of the story. His wife, who has just given birth, is presumably left alone to care for their child, an enemy of the Egyptian state. As she gazes upon her newborn son for the first time, she is struck by how truly beautiful he is. Much like God who upon taking in the beauty of creation calls it "good," she takes in the goodness of what she has created within herself. She knows that she must do whatever is necessary to protect her child from danger.

Moses's mother may have been experiencing the effects of oxytocin. Sometimes referred to as the "love hormone," oxytocin initially triggers the uterus to begin contracting. Immediately following birth, surging levels of this hormone can cause a woman to feel intense feelings of love or awe. (In my case it also caused tremendous anxiety, which took months to dissipate.) Even though the details of Moses's birth are scant, I treasure the fact that this small detail—the mother captivated by the sight of her baby—is included in the text.

In order to protect Moses, his mother hides him away from the world for three months. Some child development experts refer to this period of time in infancy as the "fourth trimester" when newborn babies are still fetus-like in many ways. While their nervous systems learn to adjust to the brightness and loud sounds of the outside world, many babies need to be held tightly to be soothed to sleep. As their digestive systems grow, newborns need to be nursed almost constantly.

I imagine Moses's mother in their hiding place as she creates a new womb-like, protective environment for her baby, perhaps fastening a discrete baby sling underneath her loose clothing, snuggling the infant Moses near her beating heart as he suckles at her breast. Surrounded by his mother's loving protection, he is shielded completely from the dangers that threaten his life just beyond the thin cloth of her milk-stained garment.

I wonder: What are the other Hebrew women doing to keep their baby boys safe? Have they all gone into hiding with their babies whose lives were spared by Puah and Shiphrah? Perhaps they designate a communal hiding area, taking shifts to care for the babies while the others go out to work so that the Egyptian officials do not notice their absence.

By the time Moses turns three months old, he has transformed from a tiny newborn to a chubby, bright-eyed, cooing baby who is now much more aware of his surroundings and no longer content to be held in secret. His mother, who has birthed two other children, knows that the protection of her body is no longer sufficient. She is physically and emotionally depleted from three months of around-the-clock efforts to keep her child fed and safe from imminent danger. No longer able to care for her son in secret, she does the only thing she can think to do. She crafts a strong basket in which to place him and prayerfully offers him to the waters of the Nile in the hopes that he might be found by someone in a better position to care for him. The woman's young daughter watches in horror (or perhaps with morbid curiosity) as her baby brother wails for his mother's arms.

Moses does find new life on the banks of the river. After some time, the daughter of the Egyptian king discovers the baby left in the basket, and despite her father's orders to kill all of the Hebrew baby boys, she has compassion on him and takes him in. When Moses's sister sees that her brother's life will be spared, she approaches the pharaoh's daughter to help: she knows someone who can nurse the baby. Mother and child are reunited for now. Despite this arrangement, the sudden yet necessary separation—the ripping apart of mother and child who have spent the last three months with bodies entwined and constantly connected—is heart wrenching. Even though Moses's mother is able to provide her son with care, she is hired help. She is no longer his rightful mother. Once again, the biological mother becomes a surrogate. The only way her child will survive is if she is willing to lose him.

This part of Moses's story reminds me of a tragic scene from the first season of *The Handmaid's Tale* television series. If you aren't familiar with the plot, part of the premise is that infertility affects most of the population, and all of the remaining fertile women are forced into sexual slavery to produce children for men in power. These women are called handmaids. In one episode a handmaid named Janine has given birth to a healthy baby girl, but the child does not belong to her because handmaids are mandated breeders for the ruling class. The baby girl is placed in the arms of the handmaid's mistress, who will raise the child as her own. The only time Janine is allowed to see her daughter is when she nurses her, but as soon as the child is weaned, Janine will never see her again. Much like Moses's story, this scene is a testament to how abusive leadership at the highest levels of government can rip families apart in the most inhumane ways.

By bringing up this example from *The Handmaid's Tale,* I hope to shift our attention back to Moses's mother and her reproductive loss, so that we may be mindful of the violence and pain, both collective and individual, that occur in this story. We must hold the tensions of the narrative: there are both things to be celebrated and things to be mourned here. We can and should laud the tremendous courage of this team of women resistors whose acts of bravery save a generation of Hebrew boys, including the one who will bring deliverance to their people. And we must not forget that while Moses survives, his mother loses everything. Nor can we forget the countless other children who lose their lives in the waters of the Nile and the families that are surely shattered by their grief. No miracle story is ever devoid of suffering.

As we navigate the tensions of pain and joy in our sacred stories and in our own lives, I pray that we might look to the model of these women in Exodus whose acts of bravery in the face of violence help hold together the humanity of their people. May we strive to be like Shiphrah and Puah, ushering in love and hope during the most turbulent of times. May we be savvy in our resistance.

1 Samuel 1:1-18

There was a certain man of Ramathaim, a Zuphite from the
hill country of Ephraim, whose name was Elkanah son of
Jeroham son of Elihu son of Tohu son of Zuph, an Ephraim-
ite. He had two wives; the name of the one was Hannah,
and the name of the other Peninnah. Peninnah had children, but Hannah had no children. Now this man used to
go up year by year from his town to worship and to sacrifice
to the Lord of hosts at Shiloh, where the two sons of Eli,
Hophni and Phinehas, were priests of the Lord.On the day
when Elkanah sacrificed, he would give portions to his wife
Peninnah and to all her sons and daughters; but to Hannah he gave a double portion, because he loved her, though
the Lord had closed her womb. Her rival used to provoke
her severely, to irritate her, because the Lord had closed her
womb. So it went on year by year; as often as she went up
to the house of the Lord, she used to provoke her. Therefore
Hannah wept and would not eat. Her husband Elkanah
said to her, "Hannah, why do you weep?
Why do you not eat? Why is your heart sad? Am I not more
to you than ten sons?"

After they had eaten and drunk at Shiloh, Hannah rose
and presented herself before the Lord. Now Eli the priest
was sitting on the seat beside the doorpost of the temple of
the Lord. She was deeply distressed and prayed to the Lord,
and wept bitterly. She made this vow: "O Lord of hosts,
if only you will look on the misery of your servant, and
remember me, and not forget your servant, but will give to

your servant a male child, then I will set him before you as a nazirite until the day of his death. He shall drink neither wine nor intoxicants, and no razor shall touch his head." As she continued praying before the Lord, Eli observed her mouth. Hannah was praying silently; only her lips moved, but her voice was not heard; therefore Eli thought she was drunk. So Eli said to her, "How long will you make a drunken spectacle of yourself? Put away your wine." But Hannah answered, "No, my lord, I am a woman deeply troubled; I have drunk neither wine nor strong drink, but I have been pouring out my soul before the Lord. Do not regard your servant as a worthless woman, for I have been speaking out of my great anxiety and vexation all this time." Then Eli answered, "Go in peace; the God of Israel grant the petition you have made to him." And she said, "Let your servant find favor in your sight." Then the woman went to her quarters, ate and drank with her husband, and her countenance was sad no longer.

Chapter 4

Challenge: Hannah

Sometimes my prayers come out sounding like I'm more interested in striking a bargain with God than I am in receiving divine guidance. Have you ever prayed for something so desperately that you've offered God a deal like this one—"I promise if you answer this prayer I will never ask for anything ever again"? Throughout my life I've turned to these helpless words in countless moments of crisis. Right about the time my grandmother Honey was diagnosed with terminal cancer, I'd begun my nightly ritual of talking to God before falling asleep. That night I prayed that if God kept her alive, I would never pray for another thing in my life.

I don't remember much about the day my grandmother died, but the memory of her funeral is clear in my mind. I'd never been to a funeral before, so all I knew about them was what I'd seen in movies or on television: scenes of bereft people dressed in black and dabbing wads of tissues to their tearful eyes. From what I'd observed, I knew that it was acceptable to cry dignified, silent tears with an occasional sniffle here and there. But as we sat in the front pew waiting for my grandmother's service to begin, I could already feel the sobs welling up within me. I began to weep into my older brother's shoulder, trying desperately to muffle the sounds of my grief so that no one would hear.

It was the first time I can remember feeling ashamed to cry in front of other people. I know that sounds ridiculous. Who wouldn't cry at their grandmother's funeral? I can't explain it. All I know is how I felt that day and how, somewhere along the way, I must have picked up the idea that crying in public—and vulnerability in general—was something to avoid, even at church.

Despite unanswered prayers for my grandmother's healing, I continued to find my way to worship services after her death. Sitting in the pew on Sunday mornings helped me feel connected to her memory. Church was the place I felt closest to her in those final months of her life, and afterwards it became a place of belonging when I felt uprooted: my grandmother had died, my parents were divorcing, and I didn't know what terrible thing would happen next.

As much as I loved church as a child, it became a complicated place once I entered middle school. Several years had passed since Honey had died, and I'd grown increasingly committed to participating in the life of the church, which included regular attendance at Sunday night youth group. Most weeks we ate pizza, played games, and goofed off during the devotions. But then one summer, our youth gatherings got more structured and serious in tone. Instead of playing games, we listened to lectures on why we should abstain from sex until marriage. Week after week I listened to terrifying presentations about the dangers of premarital sex: AIDS, pregnancy, failed relationships, and a doomed future.

After several months of delivering these weekly anti-sex lectures, the leaders of the youth group asked all of us to make a commitment to remain sexually abstinent until marriage by signing a purity pledge. Those who decided to take the pledge would stand in front of the congregation and receive gold bands to wear as reminders of the promise we had made. Needless to say, it was pretty obvious if you opted out.

The whole idea of wearing a gold band was strange to me even then. They honestly looked like actual wedding rings, like we were wed to our promise. We were instructed to keep the rings on at all times until the night of our wedding when we would give them to our respective spouses as a symbol of our preserved virginity–*our most precious gift.*

I was thirteen when I took this purity pledge. Marriage was a far-off, romantic idea, and kissing boys was still a novelty to me. With divorced parents, I was susceptible to the idea that if I followed the no-sex-until-marriage rule I'd be rewarded with a relationship that would last because it would be blessed by God. I figured it was a wise move on my part—a kind of insurance policy against future divorce.

The lectures about purity didn't stop after that. As I transitioned to high school, I found that the rules regarding abstinence were more complex than simply avoiding sex until marriage. On the surface, sexual purity was an expectation for both boys and girls—we were all encouraged to take the purity pledge—but girls had a specific role to play in ensuring that abstinence was maintained.

One of the many gender-specific "commandments" often thrown around during girls-only gatherings was to "keep the bow on the package." We were told that as girls we ought to view our bodies as gifts intended for our husbands to "unwrap" on our wedding nights. The leaders would ask us rhetorically, "Would you give someone a gift with a tear in the wrapping paper or missing a bow?" We were to keep our "packaging" completely intact, and while the specifics of what this meant were never articulated fully, the expectation was clear: as a girl I was expected to stifle my sexuality entirely until the night I got married. That included the way that I was expected to dress: no tank tops, no bikinis, no short shorts. Mind you, I grew up in a beach town with high temperatures practically year-round, so these rules regarding clothing felt particularly restrictive and difficult to follow. The rationale was always that maintaining our purity in every way would protect us from harming one another and ourselves, and we would fulfill a higher calling. By dressing modestly, we would honor God.

I prefer to follow rules, even ones that don't make sense, because I hate getting caught doing something wrong. I followed the guidance to "keep the bow on the package" by generally avoiding boys altogether and focusing on my schoolwork, though I drew the line at wearing a one piece bathing suit. As time went on, the rules felt more and more oppressive, and despite my efforts to obey them, I never felt as if I could fully measure up to what I was told God expected of me.

One summer during college I was a singer in a youth praise band that performed weekly at a thousand-person venue. Before we were scheduled to go on stage one evening, the same youth leader who'd told us years earlier to "keep the bow on the package" corralled all of the female performers in the back room. "Do you know what defrauding means?" she'd asked us. She continued, "When you dress provocatively, you are defrauding your brothers in Christ. You are leading them on sexually." Looking down at my outfit, my fitted tee shirt and jean capris, I immediately panicked that I'd inadvertently broken the modesty dress code. But I wasn't the target that particular night. Our leader looked over at one of the back-up singers, whose outfit was not much different from my own, and ordered her to go home and change her clothes, or she wouldn't be allowed to go on stage that evening.

The young woman burst into tears, understandably humiliated by being singled out for the apparent "sin" of looking too sexy. Between sobs she told us how she'd gained weight at college. She didn't need anyone telling her that her clothes were fitting her differently. She knew that. She felt that. But as a poor college student working a low-paying job at a restaurant, she didn't have any extra money to buy new clothes.

All of us gathered around her and tried to bring some solace. *You are beautiful. You have done nothing wrong. It could've been any of us.* But the damage was done. There was nothing we could say that would undo the shame she felt. I was incensed by this. I could've smacked that leader for being so vicious.

Since my departure from evangelicalism, I've become a fierce critic of purity culture that touts the kind of abstinence-only sexuality education I got in church, which has been proven to be highly ineffective against preventing pregnancy and sexually-transmitted infections (STIs) among young people. That's only partly what disturbs me about it. In a larger sense these abstinence-only messages portray sexuality as something to be avoided and re-pressed. As others have joked, these programs claim that sex is dirty and terrible—so you'd better save it for the person you love most.

These dysfunctional ideas about sex have soul-crush-ing effects, particularly for girls. As a young woman, I was taught to believe that my primary worth was in my sexual purity. If I lost it—if the bow came off the package—I surely was doomed to marital failure for which there would be no one else to blame but myself. I felt as if I was constantly on the verge of sinning just for having a body.

I've often wondered what was really at the root of this fear-based, abstinence-only education I received growing up. Discomfort with young people's sexuality, yes, but there was more to it than that. Looking back I can see how adults in my faith community discouraged young people from more than just sexual experimentation. They taught us to fear intimacy entirely.

As a teenager I was told to "guard your heart," a piece of advice pulled from the Book of Proverbs that was never fully explained to us. I took it to mean that we were to avoid any meaningful romantic connection—physical, emotional, or spiritual—that might eventually lead to heartbreak. "Purity" was more than a physical state. It demanded that we keep others out. We were cautioned against vulnerability of any kind. We were told to shut out the possibility of love, which requires vulnerability. Like the problematic framework surrounding sexuality, "guard your heart" meant keep your heart to yourself.

In recent years, some of our cultural constructions of shame, vulnerability, and courage have come to the forefront of public discourse in part because of the work done by Dr. Brené Brown, whose TED talk on vulnerability and shame has been watched by over twenty-six million people around the world. In her book *The Gifts of Imperfection* she writes, "Vulnerability is our most accurate measurement of courage."[1] Courage and vulnerability, she says, are inextricably linked.

Brown's reframing of vulnerability as a necessary component of courage helped me see more clearly what had been so off base in the messages I got from the church about sexuality, vulnerability, and love. Designing one's life around avoiding pain was not a divinely inspired goal. It was motivated by fear, not love. If the decision to avoid being vulnerable was rooted in the anxiety of being hurt, then the decision to be vulnerable in search of love and connection in spite of that fear must be rooted in bravery.

Hannah's story in the book of 1 Samuel is one of the most courageous texts in our Scriptures. She is a testament to the truth that there is great power in vulnerability. When Hannah is at her height of her depression and despair, she does not turn inward with her hurt. She does not keep her pain to herself. She does not deny or repress it. Instead she embodies vulnerability as she opens up her heart and soul before God in the temple, no matter what her critics have to say about it.

---

1   Brene Brown, The Gifts of Imperfection: Let Go of Who You Think You're Supposed to Be and Embrace Who You Are (Center City, MN: Hazelden, 2010).

HANNAH'S life circumstances are much like those of several women we have studied thus far. Like Sarai and Rachel, she struggles with infertility. According to the text, God has "closed her womb" (1 Sam. 1:5–6). And like Sarai and Rachel, Hannah's husband Elkanah has another wife named Penninah, with whom he has fathered several children. While Penninah conceives one child after another seemingly effortlessly, Hannah agonizes over her ongoing childlessness.

The interpersonal dynamics at play mirror those of Rachel, Jacob, and Leah. Hannah is deeply loved by her husband but is unable to conceive, while Penninah, the second and less preferred wife, is fertile. Like Jacob, Elkanah has no qualms about making his preference known in a public way: in the company of his entire family, he offers Hannah the best portion of meat from their annual peace offering as a demonstration of his great love for her. Understandably this display of marital preference makes Penninah immensely jealous. No matter Elkanah's personal feelings about her as a wife, she is the one who has birthed his children and who is now responsible for making sure they are fed and cared for. Why does he offer the best food to his childless wife instead of the one with several mouths to feed? With frustrations mounting, Penninah lashes out at Hannah. *Why does he love you so much when you can't even give him a baby?*

Hannah needs no reminding of her empty womb. Month after month, year after year her body's failure to conceive sends her more deeply into emotional distress. She cannot stop crying. She cannot eat. Nothing can distract her from the pain of childlessness. Elkanah wants nothing more than to bring his wife's suffering to an end, but he doesn't know what else he can do to comfort her. Exasperated, he pleads, "Hannah, why do you weep? Why do you not eat? Why is your heart sad? Am I not more to you than ten sons?" (1 Sam. 1:8). *Why am I not enough to make you happy?*

Elkanah intends his words to reassure her—that even if she never gives birth to a child, his love for her will never falter—but they fail to soothe her. Her husband's steadfast love does not fill the void of her childlessness, nor does it shelter her from the harsh realities of being an infertile woman in those times. Remember that Elkanah does not share Hannah's childlessness. He has fathered many children with Peninnah, so he does not have cause to worry about his lineage.

At least in this moment Elkanah does not stop to consider the fate that Hannah would suffer if he dies before she gives birth to a son. At risk of becoming a childless widow, Hannah's future is uncertain. Without a biological son, she has no male relative through which to inherit land or wealth of any kind. According to the tradition of levirate marriage outlined in Deuteronomy, Hannah would be forced to marry one of Elkanah's brothers and join his family (Deut. 25:5). Though I'm doubtful widowhood was at the forefront of Hannah's mind, it's worth mentioning here. However much Elkanah loves his wife, he cannot protect her against the grim future that might await her.

TO PROMOTE maternal health in my denomination I drafted language to be considered before an upcoming legislative meeting of our denominational governing body. At the time we had no public statement on maternal health, and while the ecclesial body was split on the issue of abortion, I felt confident that reducing maternal mortality was a goal behind which we all could rally.

At the time I was in my mid-twenties, single, and singularly focused on my career. Even though I cared deeply for women who faced life-threatening situations in pregnancy and childbirth, I honestly couldn't relate to them much, never having been pregnant myself. That lack of personal experience had an impact on my work in ways that I can only understand now.

In the weeks leading up to our legislative session, I shared the preliminary draft of my proposed resolution with a handful of trusted colleagues in the hopes of gaining their endorsement. While they were generally supportive of the effort, they found fault in my language and framing. For example, the opening line I'd written was something along the lines of, "God calls women to the sacred work of motherhood." This could be misconstrued to mean God calls *all* women to be mothers, something I definitely did not believe to be true. I didn't even know if it was true for me. The other trouble with this language was that it failed to recognize the many women who feel called to parent but who struggle to conceive. Where was God in that?

Infertility has not been part of my story, but it has been for friends and loved ones. Over the last few years I've cried right alongside some of my loved ones who have an unmet longing for children. Each of their experiences has taught me how complex, both medically and emotionally, infertility can be. There is so much we do not understand and so much that is downright unfair.

Infertility, the inability to conceive or maintain a pregnancy to term, affects somewhere between sixty and eighty million people worldwide.[2] In the United States one in eight couples will be diagnosed with infertility. Our reproductive systems are complex, and the causes of infertility can be hard to determine. While there are several interventions available to help couples conceive, they can be expensive and out of reach for most people, especially because insurance usually does not cover these costs. Infertility treatments like in vitro fertilization are an expensive gamble and can be grueling on a person's body. Between the steep costs, the invasiveness of procedures, and the high rates of failure, fertility treatments can take a tremendous emotional toll on a person or couple hoping to conceive.

Before becoming pregnant with my daughter, I decided to confide in only a few close friends about our hopes of starting a family. Otherwise I kept those dreams to myself. Not knowing what potential obstacles we might face on our path to conception, I figured if I couldn't control my biology, I could at least try to avoid being asked a lot of questions. Some of my friends hoping to conceive have been told by well-intended folks, "Relax. It'll happen when you stop worrying about it." File this under "Unhelpful Advice That No One Needs." Others have been told to consider "just adopting," as if there's anything simple about adoption. Besides, it completely dismisses a person's desire for a biological child. Similarly, if a woman experiences a pregnancy that she feels she cannot continue and is considering having an abortion, then saying to

2   Maya N. Mascarenhas, et al., "National, Regional, and Global Trends in Infertility Prevalence Since 1990: A Systematic Analysis of 277 Health Surveys," PLOS Medicine, December 18, 2012. http://dx.doi.org/10.1371/journal.pmed.1001356.

her, "Why don't you just place your child for adoption?" detaches us from the struggle of her decision-making by assuming adoption is what's best for her.

These attempts point to our general discomfort with other people's struggles. When we give unsolicited advice, we try to distance ourselves from their pain by suggesting there's a simple way to alleviate it. If we have not already learned this from the biblical stories we have examined thus far, matters of life and family are complex. Resist simple answers.

IN MY RESEARCH on infertility, I came across the work of social scientist Diana C. Parry, who serves as Professor of Human Rights, Equity, and Inclusion at the University of Waterloo. I find her approach to research on women's health to be refreshingly holistic, and it presses against the boundaries of the academy. For example, while conducting research about women's experiences of infertility, she decided not to compile her findings in a traditional journal article. Instead she took an innovative, imaginative approach that would better capture the complexity of what she heard. Weaving together common themes she heard throughout interviews she had conducted with more than thirty women, she crafted a collection of five short stories that were representative of the group's collective experiences of infertility. One excerpt in particular reminded me of Hannah's struggle:

I had always wanted to be pregnant and have children... I was always jealous of women who were pregnant. It did not wreak havoc on our marriage but it was stressful...I felt like I was on an emotional roller coaster. I started out each month full of hope, then I would crash down and then start all over again. It was a cycle of peaks and valleys, and I felt like I was going through it alone.[3]

This could be Hannah's own story—or the story of any woman who has struggled like her. Month after month, she feels betrayed by her body. She wonders whether something she has done in the past is preventing her from fulfilling her dreams for a family. She blames herself for her empty womb.

The emotional ups and downs of infertility can lead to depression. Studies have shown that anywhere between twenty-five and sixty percent of infertile couples experience emotional or psychological distress as a result of their condition, and the longer the duration of the infertility, the more intense their troubles become.[4] One study found that if a couple's infertility continued for longer than three years, whatever sense of optimism they may have felt at the beginning of their struggle had turned into despair.[5]

As Christians, how do we offer more support to those in our community who are struggling, often silently, with infertility? A good plan is to begin by examining the words, rituals, and practices that are already part of our communal life. Do we omit stories like Hannah's from our sacred readings—or do we lift them up in our worship? Do we speak words like "infertility" and "miscarriage" from the pulpit regularly—or do we never say them at all?

3   Diana C. Parry, "Understanding Women's Lived Experiences with Infertility: Five Short Stories," Qualitative Inquiry 10.6 (2004): 909–922.
4   Fatemeh Ramezanzadeh et al., "Survey of Relationship between Anxiety, Depression and Duration of Infertility, " International Congress Series 1271 (2004): 334–337. Web.http://www.biomedcentral.com/1472-6874/4/9#B11.
5   Ramezanzadeh et al., "Survey of Relationship."

WHEN Hannah reaches the peak of her despair, she comes to the temple for solace. Driven by desperation, Hannah prepares to bargain with God, pledging to do whatever she must in order to have a child. She prays, "O Lord of hosts, if only you will look on the misery of your servant, and remember me, and not forget your servant, but will give to your servant a male child, then I will set him before you as a Nazarite until the day of his death" (1 Sam. 1:11). Hannah promises that her future child will serve God in the temple as a Nazirite, one who vows to abstain from certain practices in order to maintain ritual purity. *If you bless me with a child, he will belong to you.* And yes, she is specific in her request: she wants a boy child, not a girl.

Like Hannah I've done my fair share of trying to convince God of one thing or another throughout my life: That my grandmother would live. That my heart would forget, if not forgive, deep betrayal committed by partners in the past. That a pregnancy test would turn out positive. That a pregnancy test would turn out negative. I've prayed for these things in the darkness, my head buried under the covers of my bed. I could speak these words to God, but I certainly didn't want anyone else to hear.

In the temple Hannah weeps and prays, prays and weeps. Her presence catches the attention of Eli, the temple priest, who watches Hannah carefully from afar. Concerned about maintaining decorum in this sacred space, Eli suspects that Hannah has had too much to drink. He confronts her: "How long will you make a drunken spectacle of yourself?" (1 Sam. 1:14). *Pull yourself together, woman. Go home and sober up. This isn't the place for you in this state.*

Eli is more concerned about maintaining appearances that with tending to the needs of the people. He approaches Hannah with a spirit of judgment instead of meeting her with compassion. Hebrew Bible scholar Yung Suk Kim writes that at a basic level, Eli is not living up to his priestly duties by treating Hannah with such condemnation.

When Hannah prays silently with her lips moving, Eli thinks Hannah is drunk. Eli, the most important religious leader in her time, does not know what is going on with her. It is an irony that Eli, who would have had a lot of experience with drunkards, does not distinguish between praying and being drunk. Maybe there was something unusual about the way Hannah prayed. Perhaps the crucial question is: if he thought she was drunk why did he not ask her the reason for getting drunk? Was she drinking her sorrows away?[6]

We all can fall into this trap of assuming the worst of those we don't understand. In thinking about our own communities, what outward expressions of pain are considered acceptable in our places of worship? What are the rules, unspoken or spoken, that we expect others to follow in our sacred spaces? What happens when someone steps outside of them?

Hannah could opt to leave the temple now. The priest has called her a nuisance. He's communicated clearly that her tears and prayers, no matter how heartfelt, are not welcome in this holy space. In this moment Hannah chooses to embody the power of vulnerability. She does

---

6   Yung Suk Kim, "The story of Hannah (1 Sam 1:1-2:11) from a perspective of han: the three-phase transformative process, "Bible and Critical Theory 4.2 (2008):26.1+. Academic OneFile. Web. Last accessed, 12 January, 2016.

not cower, nor does she apologize for disturbing the peace of the temple. With tremendous strength and resolve she responds to Eli's accusations: "No, my lord, I am a woman deeply troubled; I have drunk neither wine nor strong drink, but I have been pouring out my soul before the Lord. Do not regard your servant as a worthless woman, for I have been speaking out of my great anxiety and vexation all this time" (1 Sam. 1:15–16). *I am a person. I belong here. You will not take this from me.*

Eli sees now that he was wrong to judge this woman before knowing her story, and to his credit he acknowledges his mistake. He offers Hannah words of comfort and reassurance: *God will answer your prayer, Hannah.*

Eli doesn't know what Hannah wants from God. She divulges just enough information to disprove Eli's assumptions about her, but otherwise she withholds the details of her suffering. Vulnerability does not require us to disclose all of we who are to just anyone we encounter, religious authorities included. It's sad, though, when we feel like we can't confide in the people charged with providing care to our communities.

After receiving Eli's words of assurance Hannah returns to her husband and family with a renewed sense of hope, a restored appetite, and a lightened heart. Soon thereafter her prayer is indeed answered: she becomes pregnant and gives birth to the first of her six children, a son named Samuel who grows up to serve as a Nazarite in the temple under the guidance of Eli. Hannah keeps the promise she made to God. I should mention that this practice—of promising another's life to someone else, even God, without consent—is morally troubling.

FOR THE MOMENTS when our desperate prayers go unanswered, Hannah's time with God in the temple may bring us some comfort. We do not have to hide or silence our pain from God. Hannah reminds us that no matter what we may be experiencing, we are worthy of God's love. What if, instead of feeling apologetic for our tears, we claimed them as sacred? Let us embrace our weeping as we struggle to find hope. Let us embrace one another's pain and hold it with tenderness. Let us cling to the truth that God faithfully journeys alongside us through it all.

Ruth 1:1-19a; 2:1-13; 3:1-14

In the days when the judges ruled, there was a famine in
the land, and a certain man of Bethlehem in Judah went
to live in the country of Moab, he and his wife and two
sons. The name of the man was Elimelech and the name of
his wife Naomi, and the names of his two sons were Mahlon
and Chilion; they were Ephrathites from Bethlehem in
Judah. They went into the country of Moab and remained
there. But Elimelech, the husband of Naomi, died, and
she was left with her two sons. These took Moabite wives;
the name of the one was Orpah and the name of the other Ruth. When they had lived there about ten years, both
Mahlon and Chilion also died, so that the woman was left
without her two sons and her husband.

Then she started to return with her daughters-in-law from
the country of Moab, for she had heard in the country of
Moab that the Lord had considered his people and given
them food. So she set out from the place where she had been
living, she and her two daughters-in-law, and they went
on their way to go back to the land of Judah. But Naomi
said to her two daughters-in-law, "Go back each of you to
your mother's house. May the Lord deal kindly with you, as
you have dealt with the dead and with me. The Lord grant
that you may find security, each of you in the house of your
husband." Then she kissed them, and they wept aloud. They
said to her, "No, we will return with you to your people." But
Naomi said, "Turn back, my daughters, why will you go
with me? Do I still have sons in my womb that they may
become your husbands? Turn back, my daughters, go your

way, for I am too old to have a husband. Even if I thought there was hope for me, even if I should have a husband tonight and bear sons, would you then wait until they were grown? Would you then refrain from marrying? No, my daughters, it has been far more bitter for me than for you, because the hand of the Lord has turned against me." Then they wept aloud again. Orpah kissed her mother-in-law, but Ruth clung to her. So she said, "See, your sister-in-law has gone back to her people and to her gods; return after your sister-in-law." But Ruth said, "Do not press me to leave you or to turn back from following you! Where you go, I will go; Where you lodge, I will lodge; your people shall be my people, and your God my God. Where you die, I will die— there will I be buried. May the Lord do thus and so to me, and more as well, if even death parts me from you!" When Naomi saw that she was determined to go with her, she said no more to her.

So the two of them went on until they came to Bethlehem. When they came to Bethlehem, the whole town was stirred because of them; and the women said, "Is this Naomi?" Now Naomi had a kinsman on her husband's side, a prominent rich man, of the family of Elimelech, whose name was Boaz. And Ruth the Moabite said to Naomi, "Let me go to the field and glean among the ears of grain, behind someone in whose sight I may find favor." She said to her, "Go, my daughter." So she went. She came and gleaned in the field behind the reapers. As it happened, she came to the part of the field belonging to Boaz, who was of the family of Elimelech.

Just then Boaz came from Bethlehem. He said to the reapers, "The Lord be with you." They answered, "The Lord bless you." Then Boaz said to his servant who was in charge of the reapers, "To whom does this young woman belong?" The servant who was in charge of the reapers answered, "She is the Moabite who came back with Naomi from the country of Moab. She said, 'Please, let me glean and gather among the sheaves behind the reapers.' So she came, and she has been on her feet from early this morning until now, without resting even for a moment." Then Boaz said to Ruth, "Now listen, my daughter, do not go to glean in another field or leave this one, but keep close to my young women. Keep your eyes on the field that is being reaped, and follow behind them. I have ordered the young men not to bother you. If you get thirsty, go to the vessels and drink from what the young men have drawn." Then she fell prostrate, with her face to the ground, and said to him, "Why have I found favor in your sight, that you should take notice of me, when I am a foreigner?" But Boaz answered her, "All that you have done for your mother-in-law since the death of your husband has been fully told me, and how you left your father and mother and your native land and came to a people that you did not know before. May the Lord reward you for your deeds, and may you have a full reward from the Lord, the God of Israel, under whose wings you have come for refuge!" Then she said, "May I continue to find favor in your sight, my lord, for you have comforted me and spoken kindly to your servant, even though I am not one of your servants."

Naomi her mother-in-law said to her, "My daughter, I need to seek some security for you, so that it may be well with you. Now here is our kinsman Boaz, with whose young women you have been working. See, he is winnowing barley tonight at the threshing floor. Now wash and anoint yourself, and put on your best clothes and go down to the threshing floor; but do not make yourself known to the man until he has finished eating and drinking. When he lies down, *observe the place where he lies; then, go and uncover his feet and lie down; and he will tell you what to do." She said to her, "All that you tell me I will do."*

So she went down to the threshing floor and did just as her mother-in-law had instructed her. When Boaz had eaten and drunk, and he was in a contented mood, he went to lie down at the end of the heap of grain. Then she came stealthily and uncovered his feet, and lay down. At midnight the man was startled, and turned over, and there, lying at his feet, was a woman! He said, "Who are you?" And she answered, "I am Ruth, your servant; spread your cloak over your servant, for you are next-of-kin." He said, "May you be blessed by the Lord, my daughter; this last instance of your loyalty is better than the first; you have not gone after young men, whether poor or rich. And now, my daughter, do not be afraid, I will do for you all that you ask, for all the assembly of my people know that you are a worthy woman. But now, though it is true that I am a near kinsman, there is another kinsman more closely related than I .Remain this night, and in the morning, if he will act as next-of-kin for you, good; let him do it. If he is not willing to act as next-of-kin for you, then, as the Lord lives, I will act as next-of-kin for you. Lie down until the morning."

So she lay at his feet until morning, but got up before one person could recognize another; for he said, "It must not be known that the woman came to the threshing floor."

Chapter 5

Shift: Ruth

As a young child growing up in the 1980s and '90s, fear of strangers was instilled in me early and often. I remember the "stranger danger" public service announcements that aired during the Saturday morning cartoons. I also recall cautionary tales about my older brother who'd been targeted as a young boy. Once, he had picked up a candy bar in an aisle of a grocery store and found a razor blade inside. Another time he was lured into the apartment of a stranger who promised him games and toys. Miraculously, neither situation brought him any harm. Just hearing these stories was enough to instill in me an unbridled fear of unfamiliar situations and anyone I didn't know.

When I turned two, my family moved from Washington, D.C. to a small coastal town in southeast Georgia where my daily existence was essentially free of strangers. We couldn't make a quick trip to the grocery store without running into at least a half dozen people we knew.

Nearly everyone I knew in our beach town was white, wealthy, and Christian. Though my family wasn't well off or church going, I did have my whiteness, and while I felt like an outsider in some ways, I fit in more or less. It was a sheltered, homogenous existence, and as a result I developed a fairly narrow worldview. I learned to be cautious of those who didn't fit our community's implicit and explicit standards of "normal."

With all the talk of loving one another, I felt like my church only reinforced my fears of outsiders and outliers. Our youth leaders cautioned us against developing close friendships with "non-believers" and frowned upon dating such a person. "Do not be unevenly yoked," they would say, quoting 2 Corinthians 6:14. Yet they did encourage us to write down a list of people we believed needed "saving" and to pray over the list regularly, asking God to open their hearts so that they would accept Christ. In addition to non-church goers, this group included Catholics, who weren't considered to be "real" Christians.

I give thanks for my mother who worked hard to develop my empathetic side. When I complained about something a friend had done, she would urge me to consider the other person's perspective. Her response would frustrate me because what I was really after was some sympathy for myself. Over time these conversations taught me the basics of compassion and generosity, which would later help me unlearn some of the exclusionary ways of thinking I was picking up at church.

As an advocate, I believe multifaith efforts for justice are critical for moving our work forward. Our efforts are stronger when we show the breadth of support for social change in our different traditions. In January of 2018, I was in Washington, D.C. to attend a meeting with Muslim, Jewish, and Christian activists. We were gathering in-person to strategize ways that we could work together to end gender-based violence worldwide. It was just days after Donald Trump's inauguration to the presidency, and there was a palpable heaviness in the air. Being welcomed into this diverse community of advocates, who shared a commitment to making the world a safer and more just place for women, inspired me at a time when my spirit was low and I was struggling to remain hopeful.

The following afternoon, President Trump issued an executive order to stop immigrants and refugees from seven Muslim-majority countries from entering the United States. I was stunned by the news. How could it be possible that in the exact same city, mere miles from where I'd gathered with Muslim colleagues to discuss ending gender-based violence, something like this could happen? All I could think about were the colleagues with whom I'd met just the day before and how it must feel to live with an administration that denied their goodness—their very humanity.

I believe that this kind of systemic prejudice can exist only when we refuse to know one another, because building relationships is the antidote to othering. As we bridge the gaps that divide us and create meaningful connections with each other, we begin to heal ourselves from the toxic ideas about the "other" that prevent us from seeing the sacred worth in us all. Part of this healing work is recognizing and mourning how much love, joy, and goodness we may have missed because we let fear stand in the way of building relationships.

The story of Ruth and Naomi is one I have long treasured as a powerful testament to the possibilities of human relationships that are formed across difference. I know many other women who have turned to this text as a model for female friendship, commitment, and love. As I will explain further, the differences between Ruth and Naomi are significant—and at times they can play a divisive role in their relationship—but these two women do not allow their differences to stop them from banding together for their collective survival and well-being.

THE MOST commonly quoted passage from the book of Ruth is when she says to Naomi: "Do not press me to leave you or to turn back from following you! Where you go, I will go; where you lodge, I will lodge; your people shall be my people, and your God my God" (Ruth 1:16). It's a beautiful text of commitment between two women, and it's one of my favorite Scriptures.

I'm often reminded of this passage when I hear the theme song for *Gilmore Girls*, a series that—I kid you not—I've watched and re-watched dozens of times. The show focuses on the complexities of mother-daughter relationships, and the dialogue is delightfully quick and witty. Carole King wrote and performed the theme song "Where You Lead," which she has said in interviews was inspired by this very passage from the book of Ruth.

Outside of *Gilmore Girls* viewing, the time I most often hear this Scripture quoted is during wedding cere-monies. On the one hand, it's refreshing not to hear the tried-and-true but arguably overused passage from 1 Corinthians 13 about all of the attributes of love. But in a recent conversation with my friend and Kindreds podcast co-host Ashley Peterson, she said something that struck me as important. "There are so few passages about female friendship in the Bible," she said. "When we quote this at weddings, don't we lose something when we make it all about romantic love?"

We do lose something, I think. The relationship Ruth and Naomi share is quite different from a marriage. Throughout ancient times and still today, marriage is a social and legal contract that permits access to certain rights and protections. Ruth and Naomi have none of these. Their bond is about survival. They need each other because frankly, they don't have anyone else.

Their story begins with unfathomable tragedy. Naomi and her two daughters-in-law have lost their husbands from causes unknown. As widows with no remaining male relatives, they are in a precarious situation: they have no rights, no protections, and no access to any sort of livelihood. Of the three women, Naomi is the most vulnerable. Not only is she less likely to remarry due to her age, but unlike Ruth and Orpah, Naomi isn't living in her homeland at the time. She is from Judah; Ruth and Orpah are from Moab.

Naomi's only option if she wants to survive is to return to the remaining family she has back in Judah. If the women hope to stay together, Ruth and Orpah must migrate with her. Both daughters-in-law are fiercely determined to remain with Naomi. They want to travel with her, but Naomi is concerned for their futures in Judah. She questions if this is what will be best for them in the long run. If they stay in Moab, they have a better chance of remarrying and moving forward in their lives.

As much as it pains her to say this, Naomi urges her daughters-in-law to return to their families: "Go back each of you to your mother's house. May the Lord deal kindly with you, as you have dealt with the dead and with me. The Lord grant that you may find security, each of you in the house of your husband" (Ruth 1:8–9). There is no animosity in Naomi's heart. There is only love. She gives them her blessing. *Don't worry about me. You are young. Start your lives over.*

The women weep. Again, Ruth and Orpah insist that they want to stay together, but Naomi pleads a second time for them to return home:

> *Turn back, my daughters, why will you go with me? Do I still have sons in my womb that they may become your husbands? Turn back, my daughters, go your way, for I am too old to have a husband. Even if I thought there was hope for me, even if I should have a husband tonight and bear sons, would you then wait until they were grown? Would you then refrain from marrying? No, my daughters, it has been far more bitter for me than for you, because the hand of the Lord has turned against me* (Ruth 1:11–13).

She makes it heartbreakingly plain: No matter how much they love one another, no matter how much grief they have shared, no matter how strong their bond—they won't be able to be a family. The patriarchal laws and customs of the land refuse to recognize what we can see is true—that together they do make a family. Tragically, without men in the mix, they are unable to access what they need to live.

Orpah and Ruth must each make her own decision about the future. Neither path will be easy. In the end Orpah hesitatingly decides to heed Naomi's advice, and she returns to her childhood home. Ruth decides to stay. She knows all that it will cost her—giving up her customs and practices for those of a new land. She is firm in her decision: her life is tied to Naomi until the end. "Where you die I will die," she says (Ruth 1:17).

I wish we talked more about Orpah's decision to remain in Moab. Do we view her as less committed or loyal to her family because she decides to return home? In the end it's about survival. Orpah believes what Naomi says: that her chances are best if she parts ways with them, no matter how much it pains her.

I wonder, too, whether we make a mistake in romanticizing Ruth's commitment to Naomi. Let's revisit the passage: "Do not press me to leave you or to turn back from following you! Where you go, I will go; where you lodge, I will lodge; your people shall be my people, and your God my God" (Ruth 1:16). Is it possible that something more than family loyalty motivates Ruth to stay with Naomi? Perhaps returning to her mother's house, as Naomi suggests, is not a viable option for her. We can't know why wandering into a strange land is the best—and perhaps the only—choice available to Ruth. But for better or worse, that is the decision she makes.

AS YOU READ through the book of Ruth, you may notice a peculiar theme that arises again and again. The writer constantly identifies Ruth as a Moabite. In the first chapter alone, there are four mentions of her nationality. Most absurdly in verse 22 of the first chapter, Ruth is redundantly referred to as "the Moabite...who came back with [Naomi] from the country of Moab." In other words, Ruth doesn't belong here in Bethlehem.

I took a course in divinity school called "Gender, Sex, and Power in the Books of Ruth and Esther." (Yes, it was as fascinating as you'd think.) While many of the details of that class have since faded from my memory, I distinctly remember a class discussion of how often Ruth is identified as a foreigner. The writer obviously wants to reinforce the point that no matter how many wonderful qualities she may have, Ruth is an outsider. She is a stranger who despite all her attempts to assimilate in the land of Judah doesn't truly belong. By pointing out her difference, the author's message is clear: Ruth is not one of us.

At its core, the Book of Ruth is an immigration story. The author's tireless efforts to "other" her reminds us that the kind of debates we have today about immigration are nothing new. Arguments over immigration policy have dominated the U.S. political landscape for decades, but they have grown increasingly vicious in the era of Donald Trump's presidency. The question "Whom shall we welcome?"—or more accurately "Whom shall we exclude?"—is at the center of these debates, even if not stated explicitly. They are manifestations of fear fueled by white supremacy, American superiority, and Christian exclusivity: we will lose something if we welcome the (wrong) stranger into our midst.

Debates over immigration are happening all over the world, not just in the United States. Around the globe, migration has been rising sharply over the last fifteen years. According to United Nations (UN) estimates, more than 244 million people are currently living in a different country from the one in which they were born, although much of this increase we can attribute to overall global population growth and globalization. As it turns out, the percentage of migrants as part of the total migration has remained steady at three percent over the last twenty years, according to UN reports.[1]

North America ranks third highest for migrants with more than fifty-four million living on the continent; approximately forty-seven million of them are now living in the United States. Although the majority of migrants move within the same general geographic area, nearly all migrants to North America come from faraway regions. The process of moving to a new country is filled with risks and dangers, particularly for those living in poverty, and those risks only increase for those traveling long distances when returning home is no longer a feasible option.

LIKE MANY immigrants arriving in a new land, Ruth has no money and few resources. She must rely on the generosity of strangers for her survival. The first thing she must do is secure a food source. She plans to visit the fields that have been harvested for the season and gather up any remaining fruits and vegetables the workers have left behind. She says to Naomi, "Let me go to the field behind someone in whose sight I may find favor" (Ruth 2:3). She chooses the crops belonging to Boaz, a distant relative of Naomi's, hoping that there she might find kindness, or at least safety.

Today the United States, millions of farm workers, most of them immigrants, work to plant and harvest the crops that fuel the twenty-eight billion dollar agricultural industry each year. Some workers travel back and forth

---

1   United Nations, Department of Economic and Social Affairs, Population Division, International Migration Report 2015: Highlights, 2016. http://www.un.org/en/development/desa/population/migration/publications/ migrationreport/docs/MigrationReport2015_Highlights.pdf.

seasonally between the U.S. and Mexico while others remain in the U.S. year-round, often moving with the harvests. Since many farm workers do not have legal documentation and are working "off the books," they have no access to the labor protections that regulate pay and working conditions. Much like domestic workers who tend to people's homes and families, many farm workers do not have access to fair wages, safe environments, or freedom from violence and harassment while working. Like Ruth, they are at the mercy of those who own the fields.

Women make up about a quarter of all farm workers in the United States.[2] While all laborers are at risk of harassment and mistreatment, women bear the brunt of sexual harassment and violence on the farms. A whopping sixty percent of women who work the fields report that they have been sexually harassed at work.[3] Think about the immense imbalance of power: farm workers are dependent upon their employers for wages to feed their families and sustain their lives. They can't risk losing their primary source of income. Without access to the legal or social services systems, they have no choice but to find a way to endure the harsh, dehumanizing conditions of the farm.[4]

Had Ruth chosen any other field, she might have encountered abuse, violence, or harassment while gathering food. After her first day working, Boaz assures her that

2   U.S. Department of Labor, Findings from the National Agricultural Workers Survey (NAWS) 2013-2014, December 2016. https://www.doleta.gov.
3   Jose R. Padilla and David Backon, "Protect Female Farmworkers," New York Times, January 19, 2016.
4   Human Rights Watch, Cultivating Fear: The Vulnerability of Immigrant Farmworkers in the US to Sexual Violence and Sexual Harassment, July 11, 2011.

he has spoken with the young male workers and warned them not to bother her as she works, though he still cautions her to keep her distance from them (Ruth 2:9). From what we know, Ruth is fairly well protected. But most migrant workers today do not have the watchful eye of a wealthy landowner, let alone a relative, to ensure that they can work safely and freely. In too many instances the one in charge *is* the abuser.

ALTHOUGH this is book about women's stories, we need to talk about Boaz.

In my high school girls' Bible study group I remember the leaders speaking about Boaz as the ideal partner and "Godly man." They encouraged us to "wait for your Boaz." Rather than spending our time dating, they told us to pray for our future husband and cautioned against settling for anyone less than "Boaz material."

From those discussions you would've thought that this whole story was not really about Ruth at all (never mind that the book is named after her). According to them, Boaz is the real hero—the benevolent landowning beau, the kind rich man who rescues Ruth like a damsel in distress. He gives her everything she needs. He takes care of her. It sounds like a romanticized, biblical version of the same old fairytale story I'd heard again and again as a child.

In my opinion the phrase "wait for your Boaz" hardly describes Ruth's actions. She is anything but patient and hardly passive. Waiting around to be rescued is not a luxury she can afford. At every turn, Ruth is proactive and strategic in securing her survival and making sure Naomi is cared for too, even when it requires her to jeopardize her personal safety. Let's not forget about the immense power differences between Boaz and Ruth. His fields, after all, are her food source.

There are limitations—possibly even dangers—to reading intent into the actions of any biblical figure, but for a moment let's entertain the possibility that Boaz is moved by more than pure benevolence when he breaks social customs to enter into a relationship with Ruth the foreigner. His wealth certainly gives him the flexibility to buck societal expectations. Does he like playing the role of the savior? Is he attracted to Ruth romantically or sexually? No matter his motivation in how he treats her, Boaz holds power that Ruth will never be able to access, and it's important for us to name and remember that.

These power dynamics are nowhere more obvious than in the third chapter when Ruth and Boaz are together all night on the threshing floor. One evening at Naomi's instruction and insistence, which for better or worse she trusts inherently, Ruth dresses in her best clothes, dabs perfume on her wrists, and approaches Boaz after he's had plenty to drink. Bible scholars have argued about what exactly happens between them after that when she "uncovers his feet." Some argue that this alludes to something sexual; others insist it doesn't. In either case, Ruth puts herself in a potentially harmful situation.

How many times after an incident of sexual assault have we heard the question asked, "What was she wearing?" *Then what did she expect to happen?* How many times have we heard, "Had she been drinking?" *She put herself in that situation. She should've known better.* As a culture, we tend to place the sole responsibility of sexual encounters on the women involved. From the time we are young girls, we are taught conflicting messages about our sexuality: our worth is defined by our beauty, but our ability to attract men is our greatest liability.

As much as I seek to find and celebrate the instances of biblical women's resistance and survival, I also recognize the ways in which their ability to live requires an adherence to social norms. Ruth and Naomi are forced to live in the tension of simultaneously resisting and complying with the cultural and social customs of their times. They resist by banding together, but in the end they must depend on a wealthy man—and they use Ruth's body to secure that protection.

In no way does this diminish the strength of their commitment to one another, but it does remind us that individual people cannot singlehandedly dismantle the institution of patriarchy, especially when they depend on it for their subsistence.

When I consider her story in its entirety, I see Ruth as a risk-taking, boundary-crossing survivor who explores unknown places without trepidation. She does not "wait for her Boaz" to be rescued; she seeks what she needs and takes it without apology. She finds a way to get by when the odds are stacked against her.

Ruth's story has a lot to tell us about the times when we are called to journey into new places in our lives. May she give us the courage to step into uncertainty and cling to the ones who journey alongside us, giving us the strength to persevere.

2 Kings 4:1-7

Now the wife of a member of the company of prophets cried to Elisha, "Your servant my husband is dead; and you know that your servant feared the Lord, but a creditor has come to take my two children as slaves." Elisha said to her, "What shall I do for you? Tell me, what do you have in the house?" She answered, "Your servant has nothing in the house, except a jar of oil." He said, "Go outside, borrow vessels from all your neighbors, empty vessels and not just a few. Then go in, and shut the door behind you and your children, and start pouring into all these vessels; when each is full, set it aside." So she left him and shut the door behind her and her children; they kept bringing vessels to her, and she kept pouring. When the vessels were full, she said to her son, "Bring me another vessel." But he said to her, "There are no more." Then the oil stopped flowing. She came and told the man of God, and he said, "Go sell the oil and pay your debts, and you and your children can live on the rest."

Chapter 6

Sustain: The Widow of 2 Kings

One night over a glass of wine in a nondescript hotel bar in Washington, D.C. I confessed to my friend Mary that I was struggling. Like many of the friendships I've made in adulthood, ours is long-distance—I'm on the East Coast, she's on the West. Twice a year, for many years, we attended board meetings together, and each time we would dedicate an evening to catching up, usually over cocktails. This particular evening our time to connect was disappointingly brief, and since neither of us are inclined towards small talk, we cut right to the heart of the matter.

I told her I was having trouble feeling joy in my life. At that point I was a mere four months into motherhood. Too nervous to be away from my infant daughter for that long, I'd brought her with me to the meeting, the first of many brave attempts to figure out the impossible dance of professionalism and parenthood. The transition to caring for a baby had been jolting. It threw everything in my world off balance. As I scrambled to find a way to right myself, I began to question a lot of things in my life, especially how I was spending my daytime hours.

I felt drained. For weeks I'd attributed this listlessness to the inevitable but nonetheless shocking impact of constant sleep deprivation. But as my daughter's sleep (thankfully) improved, the haze I'd been walking around in had begun to clear a bit, and I was increasingly suspicious that it was really my day job that was weighing on me. What for years had given me a sense of purpose and fulfillment now felt stifling and restrictive. I felt trapped.

Mary listened attentively, taking sips of her gin and tonic as I waffled over what to do. After I'd laid out all of my conflicting feelings over whether to stay in my current position or search for a new one, she said to me, "Katey, you're much too young to stay in a job that makes you unhappy. Have you ever thought about working for yourself?"

I'd never seen myself as an entrepreneur. I like steadiness—and a steady paycheck. I'd always worked for one institution or another, non-profits mostly, but at various times I'd worked at a restaurant, an accounting office, a law firm, and a high-end retail shop. Looking back now, I wasn't very good at any of those jobs. Though I was never negligent, I wasn't exactly motivated to do more than what was asked of me. The times I'd done my best work were when I had positions that granted me freedom and responsibility. In these flexible work conditions I got to set my own high expectations, which tended to far exceed those of my bosses and supervisors. Left to my own devices and ambition, I always achieved more when I was in charge of my time and workflow.

Even so, the idea of working for myself felt daunting and insurmountable, not to mention financially risky. With a new baby, our household expenses were higher than ever. But Mary's advice wouldn't leave me alone. Bit by bit, I found myself imagining what it might be like to start my own business.

I sought the counsel of friends and colleagues to confirm that if I made this move I wouldn't be doing something foolish. I spoke with several other women who had become entrepreneurs out of sheer necessity. Some of them had been fired from their jobs or were forced to leave toxic work environments that were causing them stress and, in the most extreme example, anxiety-induced heart palpitations. Many of them were mothers like me who had families to support, oftentimes on their own.

I need to acknowledge how privilege allowed me to pursue my entrepreneurial path. Most people never have the opportunity to work for themselves because they cannot afford the economic uncertainty that comes with it. Although my family took a financial hit when I left full-time employment, we have never struggled to pay our bills or put food on the table. The solution to toxic workplaces ought not to be for everyone to abandon their jobs. We should be working collectively to address systemic issues of employee mistreatment and abuse, including those that go virtually unchecked in justice organizations that tout the noblest of missions.

In learning my story, you may think that I was foolish to give up a well-paying job. I get that—because some days I think the same thing. My work is harder than it's ever been and the payoff isn't immediate. But looking back at how miserable I was before I left my old job, I can't imagine how I would be feeling now had I not taken the risk when I had the opportunity to do so.

As a business owner I've made countless mistakes along the way. I've filled out financial paperwork incorrectly and had to redo it. I've taken on projects not worth my time and had to eat my losses. I often feel pulled in many different directions and sometimes long for simpler days. I tell people that if I had known how difficult this would be, I would never have done it. I suppose that's true of many of life's biggest, most rewarding challenges.

Early on I wished someone would just tell me what to do. I wanted someone to hand over the blueprint to building a successful business and direct my steps accordingly. But I realize now that would have been another version of me working for someone else. If I wanted to create something meaningful, there was going to be a lot of unglamorous, uncompensated work involved—and I was going to have to figure it out on my own.

At the same time I've also learned that none of us can succeed without community—without the confidence and encouragement of those who believe in us. When we go to the elders in our lives for words of wisdom, and we plead for them to fix our problems, they hold our hands, wipe our tears, and offer us the words of assurance we most need to hear: "You've got this."

THE STORY found in 2 Kings 4, often known as the story of the Widow and the Miracle of Oil, is a story of triumph and survival. It's a testament to how in times of crisis women can identify the resources available to them, turn to their communities for support, and step out boldly in faith.

This passage from Scripture was not one I'd originally considered including as a chapter, but one day shortly after turning in my book proposal, I was speaking with my friend Vanessa about my upcoming plans to launch a small business, something she herself had done when her children were small. When I told her about this book project, she urged me to include the widow's story as a biblical example of female entrepreneurship.

We know little about the widow's late husband, but we know that he was a follower of the prophet Elisha. He may have been a good husband and an attentive father, though perhaps not. We do know that he accumulated a certain amount of debt. Now, that debt is jeopardizing the well-being of his family. After he dies, his wife has no way to repay what is owed. A creditor threatens to enslave the widow's sons if he does not get his money back soon.

We know from Ruth and Naomi's story as well other biblical texts that widows are one of the most vulnerable populations in society. The same is true today as it was thousands of years ago. In many places widows aren't able to inherit their husbands' property or wealth. For the widow in 2 Kings, the socioeconomic infrastructure does not support her ability to earn a living wage. And yet she is still culpable for the debts incurred by her husband during his lifetime.

Faced with the threat of her sons' enslavement, she seeks the help of Elisha. She begins by acknowledging her husband's faithfulness to God: "You know that your servant [my husband] feared the Lord" (2 Kings 4:1). But his service to God has not offered her or her children any protection. Unless she finds a way to scrounge up enough money to repay her husband's creditor, she will lose her sons.

Surely Elisha knows at least something of her situation. The news of her husband's death would have made it to him by now. I wonder why the faith community hasn't already come together to support her. I suppose we all know how even the most faithful followers of God can get caught up in the work of piety at the expense of those in need.

Interestingly, no commentary that I've found on this passage addresses the lack of support that leads the widow to approach Elisha in the first place. When as readers we know a miracle is coming, we easily skip over the circumstances that created the need for such a miracle to occur.

After hearing the widow's plea, Elisha's response comes off a bit flippant and dismissive. "What shall I do for you?" he asks (2 Kings 4:2). He does not have an easy solution to her problem. What she needs is money, and he has none to spare.

Elisha becomes a thought partner in helping the widow solve her problem. He asks her to consider what she has in her possession that may be of some value. At first she comes up with nothing. Then she remembers a single jar of oil that she does have. Alone, this resource is not enough to protect her family, but with Elisha's help, it will serve as the sustenance for their long-term survival.

TIME and time again, our sacred texts call us to take care of widows and orphans. Psalm 68:5 refers to God as the "defender of widows." Some time ago I learned that in the Hebrew Bible an orphan is considered to be a fatherless child, not a parentless one. Without the protection of a father or a husband, orphans and widows are most in need of the community's care and concern.

When I first began to study 2 Kings 4, I pictured the widow as being in her later years with a head full of grey hair and the lines of a life well-lived marking her face. That's probably because most of the widows I know are women in my church who are in their seventies, eighties, and nineties—a testament to the statistic that women on average outlive men. When they became widows, their children were grown and out of the house.

Then I thought about the fact that this widow's children are still living at home with her. Presumably they are not yet married, nor are they earning incomes that could pay off their father's debt. In all likelihood she is not advanced in her years, but is in fact a relatively young woman when her husband dies and leaves her alone to care for children who depend on her entirely.

Though most women who lose their partners are older, widowhood affects women of all ages, including mothers still raising young children like the widow in our story. Today more than 584 million children under the age of eighteen are being raised by widowed mothers.[1] In places where disease and war are rampant, and where girls marry at very young ages, women tend to lose their husbands earlier in life. In Afghanistan, for example, widows make up about seven percent of the total population. On average, widows are thirty-five years old and have young children in their care.[2]

Worldwide there are an estimated 258 million widows.[3] The Loomba Foundation estimates that around fifteen percent of all widows live in extreme poverty, surviving on less than two dollars a day. Many of these women were already living in poverty before losing their

---

1   The Loomba Foundation, Global Widows Report: A Global Overview of Deprivation Faced by Widows and Their Children, March 2015.

2   Deborah Zalesne, "Helping Afghanistan's Widows," New York Times, December 24, 2007.

3   The Loomba Foundation, 2015.

husbands, but now they endure even more severe financial distress. Even in less extreme cases, the loss of a husband's income can be financially devastating for women who previously were economically secure.

The Bible's call to care for widows and the orphans is needed just as much now as it was in those times. Widows continue to be marginalized socially and economically, and on the whole they lack the financial support they need to move forward in their lives.

Gender bias in inheritance practices is a major barrier for widows seeking financial stability. In many parts of the world women continue to lack rights to property, so they cannot inherit the assets that they owned together with their husbands. As a matter of custom in Ghana, for example, when a man dies the role of distributing his property and assets lies with the wider family rather than with his wife and children. Though there are legal protections in the constitution for women to receive part of the inheritance, in practice these social customs often supersede the law, and widows are left with little or none of the assets they owned with their spouses.[4]

The challenges of widowhood extend far beyond financial devastation. Widows can be severely stigmatized in their communities. In certain instances, they may be suspected of having been involved somehow in the death of their husbands. Widows are expected to participate in humiliating and coercive "cleansing" rituals, which may include being forced to have unprotected sex with a relative or even a complete stranger.

---

4   Augustina Akoto, " 'Why Don't They Change?' Law Reform, Tradition and Widows' Rights in Ghana," Feminist Legal Studies, 21(3) 2013: 263–279.

One of the common cultural norms surrounding widowhood still practiced today is levirate marriage or "wife inheritance," which we find outlined in certain biblical texts. When a man dies, the widow is married off to one of his male relatives. Presumably, given the unjust practices around inheritance and property ownership, this has the potential to offer at least some protection to a widow and her children. On the other hand, we must recognize how the practice of levirate marriage is another form of forced marriage that puts women at physical, mental, and financial risk.

Like the widow of 2 Kings, many women today who lose their husbands have few options for taking care of themselves and their families. One element that runs throughout both the developed and developing world is an overall lack of attention paid to the status of widows in government social programs. No matter where they live, widows and their needs are essentially invisible in these systems.

THIS biblical story of a widow and her single jar of oil centers around a miracle. The prophet Elisha takes the one remaining resource in the widow's possession and multiplies it to provide enough income for her to pay her husband's debt, save her sons from slavery, and sustain her family.

Though Elisha provides the means and the guidance, the widow is the one who must see this story to its end. She and her children have a long journey ahead of them as they learn how to start and run a sustainable business together. Even with the surplus of valuable oil on their hands, they don't have all of the resources they need to carry out their work. The continuously flowing oil is useless if it cannot be properly contained, measured out, and sold. Elisha advises the widow to gather up as many empty jars as she can find, so she and her sons approach their neighbors and strangers alike, asking to borrow empty jars and other vessels.

As with any new business endeavor, theirs is not without risk. Oil is a precious commodity, and as they fill up jar after jar, their potential fortune grows. Elisha specifically instructs them to carry out their work behind closed doors. He doesn't want anyone robbing them of the one resource they have.

When the last of the jars has been filled to the brim and the oil stops flowing, the widow returns to Elisha for one last piece of advice. Now that she has all of this oil, what should she do next? He tells her to sell it, pay off her debts, and live off the rest. Again, the details are left for her to figure out. How will she sell the oil effectively? What is a fair price for a jar? How will she continue to protect her goods from those who wish to exploit her? Now that she has the resources to start a business, she has to learn quickly how best to use them.

This passage is the first and last concerning the widow and her sons. We could assume that all ends well for her: she pays her creditors, starts a successful business, and finds a way to maintain her family's well-being. But in truth we don't know that. She has one opportunity to make it in this life, and she cannot fail. There is nothing—and no one—on whom she can fall back.

In so many ways this story represents the millions of women today living as widows and single moms, many of them in dire poverty. What they need is not merely a handout, though that would be a start. What they really need is the opportunity to be financially self-sufficient by having access to adequate resources.

In her reflection on this passage, Dorothy Aokoto, a Ghanaian theologian, describes the different kinds of "indebtedness" that women inherit when their husbands die. For women to heal, Aokoto says, they must be active participants in their own processes of recovering from these wounds. She writes, "As African women we must take up the challenge and intentionally free ourselves from the chains of culture and religion, like the widow of 2 Kings 4:1–7."[5]

The story of the widow and her oil is a model of female persistence and tenacity in the midst of life's most trying circumstances when everything sacred to her is at risk. After the tragic death of her husband, she refuses to let financial ruin tear her family apart. She holds her religious leader accountable and asks for his help in finding her way forward. She does not wait to be saved. She finds a way to save herself.

When we think all is lost and that we have nothing left, may we search for that single bottle of oil we still possess—the hope that cannot be extinguished, the sustenance that keeps us moving forward, and the courage that nudges us to take the leap.

---

5   Dorothy BEA Akoto-Abutiate, *African Theology/ies: A Contemporary Mosaical Approach* (Bloomington, IN, AuthorHouse: 2014), 67.

Luke 1:13-56

In the days of King Herod of Judea, there was a priest named Zechariah, who belonged to the priestly order of Abijah. His wife was a descendant of Aaron, and her name was Elizabeth. Both of them were righteous before God, living blamelessly according to all the commandments and regulations of the Lord. But they had no children, because Elizabeth was barren, and both were getting on in years. Once when he was serving as priest before God and his section was on duty, he was chosen by lot, according to the custom of the priesthood, to enter the sanctuary of the Lord and offer incense. Now at the time of the incense offering, the whole assembly of the people was praying outside. Then there appeared to him an angel of the Lord, standing at the right side of the altar of incense. When Zechariah saw him, he was terrified; and fear overwhelmed him. But the angel said to him, "Do not be afraid, Zechariah, for your prayer has been heard. Your wife Elizabeth will bear you a son, and you will name him John. You will have joy and gladness, and many will rejoice at his birth, for he will be great in the sight of the Lord. He must never drink wine or strong drink; even before his birth he will be filled with the Holy Spirit. He will turn many of the people of Israel to the Lord their God. With the spirit and power of Elijah he will go before him, to turn the hearts of parents to their children, and the disobedient to the wisdom of the righteous, to make ready a people prepared for the Lord." Zechariah said to the angel, "How will I know that this is so? For I am an old man, and my wife is getting on in years." The angel replied, "I am Gabriel. I stand in the presence of God, and I have been sent to speak to you and to bring you this good news. But now, because you did not believe my words, which will be fulfilled in their time, you will become mute, unable to speak, until the day these things occur." Meanwhile the people were waiting for Zechariah, and wondered at his delay in the sanctuary. When he did come out, he could not speak to them, and they realized that he had seen a vision in the sanctuary. He kept motioning to them and remained unable to speak. When his time of service was ended, he went to his home. After those days his wife Elizabeth conceived, and for five months she remained in seclusion. She said, "This is what the Lord has done for me when he looked favorably on me and took away the disgrace I have endured among my people."

In the sixth month the angel Gabriel was sent by God to a town in Galilee called Nazareth, to a virgin engaged to a man whose name was Joseph, of the house of David. The virgin's name was Mary. And he came to her and said, "Greetings, favored one! The Lord is with you." But she was much perplexed by his words and pondered what sort of greeting this might be. The angel said to her, "Do not be afraid, Mary, for you have found favor with God. And now, you will conceive in your womb and bear a son, and you will name him Jesus. He will be great, and will be called the Son of the Most High, and the Lord God will give to him the throne of his ancestor David. He will reign over the house of Jacob forever, and of his kingdom there will be no end." Mary said to the angel, "How can this be, since I am a virgin?" The angel said to her, "The Holy Spirit will come upon you, and the power of the Most High will overshadow you; therefore the child to be born will be holy; he will be called Son of God. And now, your relative Elizabeth in her old age has also conceived a son; and this is the sixth month for her who was said to be barren. For nothing will be im-

*possible with God." Then Mary said, "Here am I, the servant
of the Lord; let it be with me according to your word." Then
the angel departed from her.*

*In those days Mary set out and went with haste to a Judean
town in the hill country, where she entered the house of
Zechariah and greeted Elizabeth. When Elizabeth heard
Mary's greeting, the child leaped in her womb. And Elizabeth was filled with the Holy Spirit and exclaimed with a
loud cry, "Blessed are you among women, and blessed is
the fruit of your womb. And why has this happened to me,
that the mother of my Lord comes to me? For as soon as
I heard the sound of your greeting, the child in my womb
leaped for joy. And blessed is she who believed that there
would be a fulfillment of what was spoken to her by the
Lord." And Mary said, "My soul magnifies the Lord, and
my spirit rejoices in God my Savior, for he has looked with
favor on the lowliness of his servant. Surely, from now on
all generations will call me blessed; for the Mighty One has
done great things for me, and holy is his name. His mercy
is for those who fear him from generation to generation. He
has shown strength with his arm; he has scattered the proud
in the thoughts of their hearts. He has brought down the
powerful from their thrones, and lifted up the lowly; he has
filled the hungry with good things, and sent the rich away
empty. He has helped his servant Israel, in remembrance of
his mercy, according to the promise he made to our ances-
tors, to Abraham and to his descendants forever." And Mary
remained with her about three months and then returned to
her home.*

John 2: 1-11

On the third day there was a wedding in Cana of Galilee, and the mother of Jesus was there. Jesus and his disciples had also been invited to the wedding. When the wine gave out, the mother of Jesus said to him, "They have no wine." And Jesus said to her, "Woman, what concern is that to you and to me? My hour has not yet come." His mother said to the servants, "Do whatever he tells you." Now standing there were six stone water jars for the Jewish rites of purification, each holding twenty or thirty gallons. Jesus said to them, "Fill the jars with water." And they filled them up to the brim. He said to them, "Now draw some out, and take it to the chief steward." So they took it. When the steward tasted the water that had become wine, and did not know where it came from (though the servants who had drawn the water knew), the steward called the bridegroom and said to him, "Everyone serves the good wine first, and then the inferior wine after the guests have become drunk. But you have kept the good wine until now." Jesus did this, the first of his signs, in Cana of Galilee, and revealed his glory; and his disciples believed in him.

Chapter 7

Risk: Mary

The first place I ever saw a nativity play was in the fellowship hall of the First Southern Baptist Church down the street from my childhood home. As I've shared before, my family wasn't the church-going type, and the only reason we were there was because my brother's friend was playing the part of one of the shepherds. I was around five or six years old at the time, and I hadn't the slightest clue as to what the play was about or even who Jesus was.

What I did know was that the girl playing Mary must have been special because she got to hold a baby. As the youngest child in my family, the closest I ever got to an infant was my bald Cabbage Patch doll named Rosie, more accurately referred to by me as "Wosie." As much as I cherished that doll, she was pretty lackluster when compared to a real baby.

Throughout the play I sat up as straight as I could in the squeaky metal folding chair, craning my neck to peer through the rows of grown-ups sitting in front of me in the hopes that I might catch a glimpse of the baby's face. You can imagine my disappointment when my mom later shared with me that the girl playing Mary had only been holding a doll.

Years—and many nativity plays later—I attended a

church that hosted a live, walk-through nativity each year during which the sanctuary and surrounding buildings were transformed into the ancient city of Bethlehem. They even managed to bring camels in for it, though I have no idea from where. In a small town like that, it was a great source of entertainment, and people flocked from all over to see it.

As you can imagine, the stakes were quite high for those church members playing the holy family. That Christmas Eve I saw that a young girl I'd babysat only a few years earlier was playing the part of Mary. She was dressed in an iconic blue robe fashioned from an old sheet, and as she and the boy playing Joseph made the long, slow walk to the front of the congregation, she delicately carried a swaddled bundle in her arms while the church's music director tenderly played "Away in a Manger." It was a very sweet scene.

When they reached the front of the church, the young girl leaned down to place the baby gently in the wooden manger, but somehow she misjudged the side of it and ended up smacking the poor baby Jesus in the head. (Don't worry; it was a doll). We might've missed her error entirely had it not been for the look of panic on her face—or for the loud thumping sound of the hard plastic meeting wood that reverberated throughout the sanctuary. With flushed cheeks and an averted gaze, she dashed to the pew where her family was sitting. With that, I was over my unmet desire to play Mary in the Christmas play.

Head injuries and other potential mishaps aside, the baby doll "stunt double" for the infant Jesus makes perfect sense. Real life babies are entirely too unpredictable to play the part in a live play. Besides, church nativities are often more about the motley crew of characters surrounding Jesus than the baby himself—the shepherds and wise men with their cotton-ball beards, the sheep with their floppy felt ears, the angels with their tinsel halos.

As much as I celebrate the opportunity to include children as storytellers in our sacred spaces, I worry about what happens when we turn the event of Jesus's birth into a children's production. The story becomes sanitized. When we clean up the birth so much, we lose touch with the reality that Jesus was born like we all are: through the bloody, sweaty, and tearful efforts of the women who give us life.

This propensity to make the birth of Jesus more palatable has a long history. If we look at various artistic depictions of the nativity throughout the ages, we see scenes that resemble illustrations from a children's book—light shining brightly upon a group kneeling before a calm, peaceful baby who looks more like a toddler than a newborn. The entire thing is like a fairy tale detached from reality.

I suppose that's why I loved the moment when the girl in my church accidentally thumped the baby Jesus—because it was so very human. Her kerfuffle reminded me that no matter how much we may try to orchestrate our lives, we are beautifully imperfect human beings with slippery hands that sometimes fumble.

Sitting in worship one Sunday, as the offering basket passed from my seatmate's hands into mine, I dropped it! Checks, dollar bills, and completed guest information cards went flying all over the pew and the floor. As I scrambled to put them back in the basket, a little boy turned to look at me with his mouth agape. Ooh, you're in trouble! He was shocked to witness a grown-up messing up in church. Well, all I can hope is that my little moment of disgrace gave everyone else enough breathing room to be their messy, flawed, and authentic selves.

Though I never dropped the baby Jesus on his head (I never had the opportunity), there were lots of painful moments I endured during my teenage years. I can recall with such vividness one instance when I misjudged a kick on the soccer field. It made such a lasting impression—the feeling of my foot sailing through the air instead of making contact with the ball, the sound of the fans groaning with pity—that I can recreate it in my mind even now.

Looking back, most of my embarrassing moments were actually quite mild, despite how intense they may have felt in the moment. They have long been forgotten by most. What about in the case of Mary, the mother of Jesus? What kind of experience did she have as a young, unmarried, pregnant girl? How did she find a way to endure the judgmental looks and the pitying glances?

The student handbook for my small high school stated that becoming pregnant was grounds for automatic expulsion. I recall only one incident in which a student carried a pregnancy to term; undoubtedly others had abortions. The school administration turned a blind eye to her boyfriend who remained enrolled there, but the young woman had no option other than to drop out once she could no longer hide her pregnancy. Despite my indoctrination in purity culture that shamed girls for having sex, I still thought the whole situation was terribly unjust. Why should she be penalized while her boyfriend continued on in school? I remember visiting her not long after the baby was born, imagining how isolated she must have felt. I wonder if she ever saw herself in Mary's story.

Sometimes I think we forget that Mary was a young girl when she became pregnant with Jesus. Our depictions of Jesus's mother often portray her as pensive and serene, her facial features more closely resembling those of a grown woman than a young adolescent girl. Do those portrayals of Mary aid us collectively in coping with some of the discomfort we feel around the story of a young girl taking on the enormous task of holding God within herself, of giving birth to God, of nurturing God as a helpless, tiny baby? What if we were to set these images aside and reimagine Mary as a girl like the ones who play her in our church nativities? What if we reflected on the reality that the baby she birthed and cared for wasn't made of plastic but was made of flesh and spirit?

AT THE BEGINNING of Luke's Gospel, the angel Gabriel shows up twice to deliver news of a surprise pregnancy. First, he visits Zechariah to tell him that after decades of infertility, his wife Elizabeth will give birth to a child. Understandably Zechariah is both stunned and confused, so he asks a very reasonable question: "How will I know that this is so?" (Luke 1:17). The angel, however, does not respond kindly to this inquiry. Refusing to provide an answer, Gabriel immediately subjects Zechariah to complete muteness for the duration of Elizabeth's pregnancy. Harsh.

Some months later Gabriel appears to Mary. Unlike Zechariah, Mary is neither terrified by the angel's presence nor elated by it. She is discerning. She understands the significance of the angel's presence, but what it will mean for her life remains unclear. Sensing unease, Gabriel reassures Mary: "Do not be afraid" (Luke 2:10). Mary has every reason to fear the creature before her. Remember what happened to Zechariah just a few verses ago.

Gabriel goes on to explain that his presence is cause for celebration: the news that he brings is good (though one could argue about just how good it might feel to Mary in the moment). Soon she will become pregnant, and she will give birth to a son. The situation, of course, is more complicated than that. Her fiancé Joseph is not the biological father. If that weren't unnerving enough, he reveals that her child will be the Son of God.

In response to this overwhelming and perplexing news, Mary asks a question not unlike the one Zechariah asks: "How can this be, since I am a virgin?" (Luke 1:34). The slight difference may be that Mary asks for an explanation instead of evidence. Interestingly, Gabriel offers her proof in response. *Your cousin Elizabeth, the one who struggled with infertility for her entire life, is six months pregnant. God is making the impossible possible.*

This explanation is sufficient for Mary to consent to the pregnancy and her central role in birthing, nurturing, and parenting the Son of God: "Here am I, the servant of the Lord; let it be with me according to your word" (Luke 1:38). *Mary says yes.*

Before I became pregnant with my daughter, there was nothing more tempting than a pregnancy test. So much of the journey towards parenting was "hurry up and wait," and those times of waiting could be agonizing. In an attempt to preserve my emotional well-being I'd pledged to wait until at least two weeks post-ovulation to take one. I more or less followed this guideline, but one morning when I was a few days short of that two-week mark, curiosity got the best of me. I took a test on a whim, half-heartedly scolding myself for breaking my own rule because I was certain I was wasting yet another expensive test. There was no way I'd get a positive result this early in my cycle.

Imagine my surprise minutes later when the slight shadow of a line appeared. I couldn't believe my eyes. Was this a fluke? Or was this an actual positive test? I couldn't quite tell. I wanted to see a line so badly—was it possible I'd created one in my own mind? This ambiguous test result had left me with more questions than answers. So I did the first thing that came to mind: I took three—yes, three!—more tests, snapped the best picture of them I could with my iPhone, and furiously texted my closest friends with a frantic request to please tell me if they saw what I saw. *Does this mean I'm pregnant?* The disbelief was too much for me to hold on my own. I needed my friends to help hold that space of hopeful uncertainty.

Mary needs community too. She may not have an ambiguous line on a pregnancy test to show, but she does have an unbelievable story to tell about her encounter with Gabriel. Think of all the life-altering information she has to process. Mary needs time and space to come to terms with what this means for her life, and she needs the support of someone else as she journeys through it. Gabriel provides the connection she needs: Elizabeth. Once the angel departs, Mary makes plans to visit her cousin.

Since becoming pregnant, Elizabeth has been living in quiet with a husband who can't speak a word. Mary's arrival must be a joy and a relief for her. Finally, after six months, she has someone she can talk to who understands what it's like when an angel brings news of an unplanned pregnancy. For three months the women live together. I love to imagine them during this time: Elizabeth's ever rounding belly and Mary's still flat. Mary moaning with each wave of nausea as Elizabeth scurries to whip up something bland to settle her cousin's stomach. The two of them sharing their hopes and fears for their future children. These months of togetherness must be incredibly sacred for them.

After confirming my pregnancy I spent the next few months feeling fairly isolated. Matt and I knew early miscarriage was common, so we decided to keep our news mostly to ourselves until I made it past the twelve-week mark. Going through the first trimester was difficult on a physical level, which I had expected, but the emotional toll of holding a secret like that even for a few weeks exhausted me. Sometimes a wave of nausea would hit me while I was in the middle of a business meeting, and I would long for someone else in the room to recognize what was going on and perhaps to offer me a ginger ale.

Thankfully I had a number of pregnant friends at the time, and they were a lifeline in those early weeks. Anytime I confided in one of them about my own pregnancy I experienced immediate relief (*someone else knows*) followed by a sense of camaraderie (*I'm not in this alone*). Those connections helped me get through my pregnancy, and now those dear women help me navigate the ups and downs of parenting. Like Elizabeth embraces Mary with joy, I give thanks for the circle of friends who embraced me with love and compassion when I needed them most.

THE WAY I thought about Mary began to shift years before I became a mother myself. In my early twenties, I moved to Washington, D.C. where I launched a grassroots maternal health advocacy campaign for a worldwide denomination. Nothing quite like this had been done before, and I spent the first year just trying to get my footing. A good portion of my work early on involved speaking to churches and other communities around the country about why people of faith should care about global maternal health and universal access to family planning. I said yes to nearly every invitation, hoping that the more practice I got, the better I'd be at delivering my message.

As a newbie to the advocacy scene, I made some strategic mistakes along the way. When I had the opportunity to speak to congregations, I often spent most of my presentation time rattling off shocking statistics and heart-shattering stories about maternal mortality, which was effective at creating a somber mood but left little room for hope to enter. At the end of each talk I could sense a heaviness in the room. I'd explained the tragedy of the situation without sharing any good news.

Over time I learned that when communities invited me to talk about creating a more just world for women and girls, they needed to learn the facts, yes, but I needed to frame my message differently. I needed to root my talk in something beyond the immediate crisis—something that would give rise to hope for a better future.

Turning to the Scriptures for inspiration, one day I came across a familiar verse that suddenly took on new meaning: "I came that they may have life and have it more abundantly" (John 10:10). In my evangelical past, the idea of "abundant life" in Christ had to do with what followed our existence on earth. Abundant life meant eternal life. But reading this Scripture in light of all I had learned about the tragedy of preventable maternal and child deaths, this verse took on new meaning for me. Abundant life, I realized, is something Jesus intends for us to experience here in this present moment.

If abundant life through Christ is meant for us now, I believe that as his followers we are called to the struggle for justice, so that every single one of us has access to the conditions and resources that allow us to thrive—to enjoy lives of abundance.

Those of us engaged in advocacy work get so wrapped up in identifying the problems and root causes of injustice that we often forget to imagine what we actually want the world to look like. In the face of tragic stories and statistics about poverty, disease, violence, and corruption, daring to dream of a better world can be challenging.

When I began my campaign on maternal health, the global statistics for maternal mortality were startlingly high—a woman died every ninety seconds from complications during pregnancy or childbirth. That number has declined steadily ever since, but not fast enough: nearly eight hundred women continue to die every day from mostly preventable complications like hemorrhaging and infection. It is geography and systemic poverty that determine a woman's level of risk in childbirth. Nearly all maternal deaths occur in the developing world where many women lack access to basic medical care. That being said, in the United States maternal mortality rates continue to climb, especially among black women who are three times more likely to die in childbirth than white women are.

One year as the season of Advent approached I was
asked to write a piece about Mary and maternal health
for a denominational publication. At first I was stumped.
How could anyone possibly write something new about
the birth of Jesus? I had very little interest in writing about
Mary at all. In my view she was a troubling model of
womanhood, embodying passivity, purity, and asexuality.

Reluctantly and skeptically, I turned to the first chap-
ters of the Gospel of Luke. As I read and re-read the story
of Jesus's birth, I began to see Mary's situation differently.
She was a poor teenager with an unplanned pregnancy.
Given her young age and the circumstances of her life,
we might consider her pregnancy high-risk. The potential for complications, possibly even death, ought not be
dismissed. Laboring in a space shared with animals leaves
her vulnerable to infection, one of the most common
causes of death for both mothers and babies. Infections
account for fifteen percent of all maternal deaths and thirty-five percent of all neonatal deaths.[1]

I see Mary in the women today who cross borders and
give birth in a land far from their homes. Remember that
she and Joseph have traveled to Bethlehem for the census.

I see her in the millions of mothers who live in areas
lacking even a single health care provider. Luke's Gospel
mentions no birth attendant who might accompany Mary
during her labor.

I see her in the adolescent girls who become pregnant

---

1   PATH, "Landscape Analysis of Maternal and Perinatal Infections,"
June 2012. http://www. http://maternalinfection.org/.

before their eighteenth birthdays without fully understanding how it happened. All of them could use the
reassuring voice of an angel. *Do not be afraid.*

When I consider the circumstances of Mary's pregnancy—young, unplanned, high-risk—and her birthing
conditions—unsanitary, possibly unattended—I strongly
believe that the miracle of nativity is not only that Jesus,
the Son of God, is born among humans, but also that
Mary survives the labor and recovers birthing him into
our world. We take this for granted. Even in the best
of circumstances, pregnancy is risky, and childbirth is
dangerous, even life-threatening. Everyday hundreds of
women lose their health or their lives while bringing new
life into existence We would be remiss not to acknowledge
these sobering realities.

WHEN I was thirty-seven weeks pregnant, Matt and I
took one final trip as a family of two to celebrate the marriage of good friends. The wedding was only about two
hours away, and we figured if I went into labor, we could
hop in the car and get back home in plenty of time to get
to the birthing center where I'd be delivering our daughter. We weren't too worried about that happening since
we'd learned in our birthing class that the likelihood of my
going into labor that early was slim. Even so, the entire
weekend I was a bit distracted with thoughts of what it
might be like to give birth in an unfamiliar place.

Mary is well into her pregnancy when she and Joseph
must make the eighty-mile journey from Nazareth to
Bethlehem for the census. Their only mode of transporta-
tion, other than walking, is to ride an animal like a camel
or a donkey. (Side note: there is no specific mention of

Mary riding a donkey in the nativity stories, but it was a common transport animal at the time.) The trip takes them close to a week. Mary and Joseph know that if she goes into labor on their journey, there is no chance they will make it back home in time. Given this journey, it's likely that they plan for Mary to give birth in Bethlehem, and they go in search of an "inn" where she will deliver their baby. There is much debate among scholars regarding what the Greek word *kataluma* in Luke 2:7 actually means, though it is often interpreted as "inn." When we read the text translated in English as "no room at the inn," images of a hotel "No Vacancy" sign might come to mind. You've probably heard sermons preached about the inhospitable innkeeper turning the young couple away, although again there is no textual evidence of this occurring.

Another way to think about this passage is to consider that Mary and Joseph have probably been in Bethlehem for some time when she goes into labor. Since Joseph is from Bethlehem, they are presumably staying with members of his family. It makes sense that "no room in the inn" means simply that the area in which they are staying is not suited for childbirth because it is too small, and they have to move to a larger area within the home.[2]

I'm not suggesting that we toss out our beloved nativity scenes with their wooden mangers surrounded by hay and adoring animals looking on simply because they aren't historically accurate. As a minister who advocates for women's health, I care less about us crafting the most logical depiction of Mary's birthing room than I do about emphasizing in our interpretations of this story that she

---

2   S. C. Carlson, "The Accommodations of Joseph and Mary in Bethlehem: Κατάλυμα in Luke 2.7," *New Testament Studies*, 56.3 (2010): 326–342.

does not have access to an ideal place to deliver her baby.

Mary's survival is something we ought to talk about more. If we stop to consider the risk to her life, could we imagine how this loss might shape Jesus's ministry? What would the life of Jesus look like without the love, care, and guidance of his mother?

There aren't many stories about Mary after the birth of Jesus, at least not in our canonical texts. But we can imagine that she, like any mother, experiences parenting challenges and joys as she raises Jesus from infancy to adulthood. I remember a preaching professor of mine commenting that the line from "Away in a Manger" (*The little Lord Jesus/No crying he makes*) shows us how uncomfortable we are with Jesus as a newborn. The vulnerability of the infant's complete dependence on his young mother makes us squirm. Can we accept God as fragile, delicate, and needy?

MARY'S PARENTING does not end when Jesus is grown. We see this most clearly in the scene at the wedding in Cana described in John 2:1–11. Mary, Jesus, and the disciples are attending a wedding celebration when she brings to her son's attention that the hosts have run out of wine, quite the social faux pas. At first Jesus is not the least bit interested in rectifying this situation: "Woman, what concern is that to you and to me? My hour has not yet come" (John 2:4). I can almost see him rolling his eyes as he says this.

Mary recognizes something in this moment that Jesus does not yet see. From the day the angel Gabriel comes to visit her, Mary knows that the son she will give birth to, care for, and raise will be set apart for the highest of callings. She endures the sleepless nights of his infancy, the tantrums of his toddler years, and the challenges of his adolescent angst knowing that one day he will fulfill his destiny. That moment has finally come.

She persists. "They have no wine," she says. She does not instruct Jesus on what he ought to do. She merely brings the dilemma to her son's attention. She creates room for opportunity and possibility, and then gives him the space to make his own decision about how he will respond. According to the Gospel of John, Jesus performs his very first miracle of turning water to wine to save a party. He has Mary to thank for that.

The more I reflect on Mary as the mother of Jesus, the more I see that there is nothing passive about her role at all. Raising a child is unpredictable and ever-changing. Parenting is a constant state of action: nurturing, guiding, reminding, explaining, advising, worrying, and anticipating. Though little of Mary's parenting story is captured in the Bible, we can see evidence of her life's work in this exchange she has with Jesus at the wedding. Mary is the bearer of holy miracles in more ways than one.

Mary says "yes" to what Pierre Teilhard de Chardin called "the slow work of God."[3] She holds fast to the vision that Gabriel revealed of what is to come for her son, and she endures many challenging years of preparing him for the moment when he is ready to live into his divine purpose fully. I give thanks for her strong and faithful nurturing of the one who gives us hope and healing today.

---

3   Harter, Michael. Hearts on Fire: Praying with Jesuits (Chicago: Loyola Press, 2005).

Luke 10:38-42

Now as they went on their way, he entered a certain village, where a woman named Martha welcomed him into her home. She had a sister named Mary, who sat at the Lord's feet and listened to what he was saying. But Martha was distracted by her many tasks; so she came to him and asked, "Lord, do you not care that my sister has left me to do all the work by myself? Tell her then to help me." But the Lord answered her, "Martha, Martha, you are worried and distracted by many things; there is need of only one thing. Mary has chosen the better part, which will not be taken away from her."

Chapter 8

Advocate: Martha of Bethany

For two years while in seminary, I lived in a house with seven roommates. If you are an older millennial like me, you may remember an MTV reality show from the 1990s called *The Real World* in which a group of strangers was selected to live in community for a period of time. The house where I lived was like a theological spin-off of that, minus the cameras and most of the fighting.

There were always people coming and going from our house. We regularly held low-key community gatherings and occasionally hosted more raucous student get-togethers. Every year my roommates and I threw a school-wide party that always got a little wild late into the night. One time two campus police officers rang our doorbell after some neighbors complained about the noise coming from our house. They asked, "What fraternity is this?" My roommate explained that we were not, in fact, associated with any fraternity, but we were a group of students from the divinity school. The officers didn't know what to make of that.

As fun as those parties were, what I enjoyed most was our weekly house dinner. Every Tuesday evening a few of us would prepare a large meal for our housemates and invited guests. We hosted admired professors, respected administrators, fellow students, and local alumni. For hours we'd sit in mismatched chairs at our oversized dining room table, laughing and talking over simple food served on chipped plates paired with glasses of cheap wine. All of us cherished that weekly ritual of opening our home to others.

Hospitality is both a spiritual practice and an art form. When we invite others into our spaces, we learn the delicate dance of anticipating and adapting to the needs and wants of others.

Soon after I met my husband Matt, I decided to take a chance and move from Washington, D.C. to North Carolina to be closer to him. I was eager to leave D.C. where housing was notoriously expensive, and all I'd been able to afford was a rented room in a dimly lit basement apartment. After years of living in cramped quarters, I was grateful to move into a house with a designated guest room and plenty of living space to host get-togethers. Matt and I love to throw parties for all of our friends—birthday festivities, holiday celebrations, and gatherings to commemorate those otherwise forgettable occasions like the end of a house renovation project or in one instance, the purchase of a new deep fryer we were itching to use.

Although I'd like to say that my desire to host others in our home comes purely from a spirit of generosity, that's not quite true. While I love the feeling of giving someone else an evening without worries or responsibilities, I feel fulfillment in another way too: it feeds my need to be productive constantly. I've often described myself as a productivity junkie who is not yet in recovery for my addiction. Nothing feels better to me than crossing items off my to-do list, and gatherings have so many tasks associated with them: planning meals, going to the store, chopping things, stirring things, cleaning things, etc. Each completed task is an ego-boosting mark of a job well done.

All of this constant doing has its downsides. Sometimes when we're hosting a large group, I almost feel like I'm having an out of body experience. It's like I'm running on autopilot, fueled by adrenaline, and rather than sitting down to chat with my guests, I end up spending a lot of the night scanning the place for glasses to refill and dirty plates to put in the dishwasher. As people begin to leave, I snap out of this trance-like state only to realize that three or four hours have passed and I can hardly remember how I spent the time. My stomach is growling because I've not eaten any of the delicious food we prepared. I'm beyond exhausted, and I'm sad that I've managed to miss the fun of it all.

This disappointment in myself can easily shift into feelings of martyrdom. When I'm overly tired and have put myself at the bottom of the priority list, I tend to slip into the downward spiral thinking pattern that sounds something like this: *Wow, we sure did a lot of work to throw this party. I wish someone else would invite us to their parties. Why are we spending so much money on everyone else? Is everyone just using us?* At the end of it, I'm miffed that we even had a party in the first place. I start to fixate on that one guest who didn't bring a bottle of wine but happily guzzled ours, or someone who promised to come but never bothered to show up. Instead of a gracious host, I become a disgruntled one. Eventually after some time has passed, I get over myself, plan another party, and tell myself that this next time will be different. I won't get resentful. I will be fully present.

The problem is that I haven't found a way to address my productivity addiction. This insatiable need to be doing something all the time seeps into every other area of my life. I tend to say "yes" to opportunities without first assessing how much energy or time I will have for them. I end up working myself into a frenetic state of feeling overwhelmed. Once, when describing this pattern to my therapist, she asked me what would happen if I were to let something fall by the wayside. "Intentionally?" I asked. I couldn't comprehend purposefully failing to complete a task. The thought alone was enough to cause me anxiety.

Where do these feelings and fears come from? For starters, our culture defines our worth by how much we are able to produce and how much money we are able to make for others and ourselves. Sadly, this push to be productive has gotten wrapped up in the language of values and morals. The Protestant work ethic, based on the theological writings of white privileged men in Europe, stresses that living out our Christian faith involves working hard at our jobs. Capitalism and the Protestant work ethic go hand in hand, and they impact all of us who live in this culture. In our society, to be good means to be productive. Those unable to produce, no matter the reason, are considered morally bankrupt and thus undeserving.

Not all work is valued equally either. Indeed, only certain kinds of productivity, namely those that earn a lot of money, are held in high regard. Unpaid and underpaid work like caretaking is highly invisible and underappreciated. It's also work done disproportionately by women, specifically low-income women, black women and other women of color, and immigrant women. Labor laws and regulations do not properly protect those who take on this virtual work that is essential to the functioning of our everyday lives.

When I think about the dynamics of gender and work in the Bible, I think of Martha of Bethany. Her experience sheds light on our perceptions of work and its value. How do we find a way to recalibrate our designation of "real" work and honor labor of all kinds? How we do engage in meaningful work while resisting the temptation to make an idol of it? Martha's story may hold some clues for us.

MARTHA OF BETHANY invites Jesus to her home, which she shares with her sister Mary and their brother Lazarus. While Martha is busy working, Mary spends time with Jesus, perhaps one-on-one with him or possibly with other disciples present. After a while, Martha gets a bit fed up with this dynamic. Rather than confronting Mary directly, Martha complains to Jesus, "Lord, do you not care that my sister has left me to do all the work by myself? Tell her then to help me" (Luke 10:40). Jesus doesn't take the bait. He responds to Martha that her sister has chosen "the better part," and he won't interfere.

As someone who feels compelled to be productive, I've always identified with Martha of Bethany's struggle. Her story was one of the few passages involving women that I did hear about regularly in church growing up. Martha's "many tasks" were described the same way in every single one of those sermons: Martha is busy preparing a meal in the kitchen while Mary sits as Jesus's feet. The preacher, always a white man, focused on the same message every time: God calls us to *being* rather than to *doing*. Be a Mary. Don't be a Martha.

I recall how the women in the congregation, most of them married with children, would nod and groan throughout these sermons. I suppose they felt convicted by them—that deep down they believed they really were a little too much like Martha when they really ought to be more like Mary.

This Martha-the-doer vs. Mary-the-listener comparison made a big splash among these women in my evangelical church when Joanna Weaver's *Having a Mary Heart in a Martha World* was released in 2000. Like me, Weaver closely identifies with Martha. In her book she paints Martha as a worker bee-type, completely dedicated to hospitality. Weaver refers to her as "the original Martha Stewart."

> *She's the Queen of the Kitchen—and the rest of the house as well...She scraps her ordinary menu of soup and bread and pulls out all her cookbooks. This, she decides, will be a banquet fit for a messiah. For the Messiah. Martha sends one servant to the field to slaughter a lamb, another to the market to pick up a few of those luscious pomegranates she saw yesterday. Like a military general, she barks commands to her kitchen staff. Soak the lentils! Pound the grain! Knead the dough![1]*

Weaver's interpretation of Luke's Gospel sounds a lot like the sermons preached in my church: Martha is too busy working to enjoy the company of Jesus. She writes,

---

1   Joanna Weaver, *Having a Mary Heart in a Martha World: Finding Intimacy with God in the Busyness of Life* (Colorado Springs, CO: Waterbrook, 2002), 33.

"The Living Room Intimacy Mary enjoyed with Jesus will never come out of the busyness of Martha's kitchen."[2] Intimacy vs. busyness. The living room vs. the kitchen. Mary vs. Martha. For Weaver, these represent an inner struggle between what she experiences as opposing forces within herself: her desire to love God and her desire for perfection. She writes, "I see the struggle I face every day when work and worship collide."[3] Pitting work against worship, and sister against sister, Weaver interprets this story as a kind of daily battle that we all must fight.

Don't work and restoration go hand-in-hand? Aren't both required for a faithful life?

Furthermore, why do folks like Weaver insist that Martha spends all of that time cooking? Why do we presume she is in the kitchen at all? There is nothing in the text that specifically places her there. The Greek word translated as "tasks" or "preparations" is *diakonian*. When this word appears elsewhere in the New Testament, it's often translated as "ministry." Author Mary Stromer Hanson astutely recognizes the not-so-subtle gender dynamics at play in how the word *diakonia* and its cognates are interpreted. When referring to the actions of men, she points out, the translation is usually deacon or minister.[4]

What if Martha's tasks are not domestic at all? What other kind of work might she be doing? There are lots of possibilities. She might be immersed in studying sacred texts. She might be preparing to speak publicly about Jesus to her community. Those "many tasks" that keep

---

2   Weaver, Having a Mary Heart, 9.
3   Weaver, Having a Mary Heart, 7.
4   Mary Stromer Hanson, The New Perspective of Mary and Martha (Eugene, OR: Wipf & Stock, 2013), 28.

her occupied may be vital to the ministry of Jesus in ways we have not considered previously. But the translation of a single word, informed by cultural assumptions about gender, influences our collective imagination so heavily that most of us have confined Martha to the kitchen.

BY RAISING the question about the nature of Martha's work, I mean to shine a light on how gender bias shapes our reading of this story. I do not wish to denigrate the importance of domestic work, something that I've already identified as terribly undervalued in our society. Neither do I wish to assert that the tasks associated with keeping a household running or hosting a guest are somehow outside the realm of ministry. Domestic work is sacred work. For that reason the interpretation of Martha at work in the kitchen is valuable because it presents us with an opportunity to reflect on how we view household work, and the value—or lack thereof—we believe it holds.

When I was in graduate school I had the opportunity to meet feminist activist Gloria Steinem while she was visiting our campus. When asked about ways to move the gender equality agenda forward, her answer surprised me. She proposed that in addition to ongoing efforts to ensure equal work for equal pay, we should adopt national policies that attribute real economic value to caregiving. For example, she proposed that parents and guardians who stay home to care for children, partners, or parents ought to receive a tax deduction or refund for doing so. In an article for *Ms. Magazine* on this topic, she wrote:

> Besides revaluing work, we also need to redefine it. Almost two-thirds of adults in the U.S. are caregivers which includes those raising children and caring for

the ill and the growing population of the elderly-yet caregiving is economically invisible. A woman or man who does it full time at home is still called someone who "doesn't work." But it's in the national interest to reward caregiving, which is often higher quality and far less expensive at home than in institutions. So why not value caregiving at replacement level — not the current tiny exemptions —and make that amount tax deductible? Or tax refundable for those too poor to pay taxes?[5]

What would our society look like if we were to value caring for one another in this monetary way? Wouldn't it transform our beliefs about this work, not only for those who care for their own families, but also for those who tend to the needs of other families in addition to managing their own?

The business of domestic work is huge. Worldwide at least fifty-three million people are employed as domestic workers. This includes nannies, cooks, drivers, home health care workers, maids, and anyone else whose work takes place primarily in other people's homes. Domestic workers have access to our most intimate spaces—where we sleep, where we bathe and dress, where we care for children and relatives, where we host guests, and where we relax. We entrust them with the responsibility of caring for these sacred places. Why, then, do we treat them so poorly?

On the whole domestic workers are severely underpaid. In the United States, workers typically make less than $13 an hour, and nearly a quarter of them receive an

5   Gloria Steinem, "Our Revolution Has Just Begun," Ms (2014, Winter) 24: 26–31.

hourly rate that is less than the state's minimum wage.[6] In addition to low pay, domestic workers are almost always excluded from receiving other benefits like paid time off, health insurance, and retirement contributions. Working conditions for domestic workers are largely unregulated and abuse is rampant. Long hours without breaks are common. Employers often ignore the conditions of their work contracts. But individual workers have little recourse. Speaking up about inadequate pay or poor work conditions could result in them being fired or, in the case of undocumented persons, being deported.

Despite the risks involved, domestic workers are coming together to stand up for their rights to fair treatment and adequate pay. They are organizing at the global level to demand the attention of policy-making bodies like the International Labor Organization (ILO) to have their work recognized as legitimate employment. In 2011, after many years of petitions from the domestic worker community, the ILO, which is part of the United Nations, passed the Convention concerning Decent Work for Domestic Workers, which includes standards for fair wages and decent work conditions with a particular emphasis on immigrant workers. Feminist scholars Eileen Boris and Jennifer N. Fish note that while international treaties are not compulsory and might not lead immediately to national policies protecting domestic workers, the significance of passing this convention should not be overlooked. Domestic worker organizations have been able to come together at a grassroots level and hold their own with the delegates of the ILO in order to get the recogni-

---

6   Linda Burnham and Nik Theodore, HomeEconomics: The Invisible and Unregulated World of Domestic Work, National Domestic Workers Alliance, 2012. www.domesticworkers.org.

tion they deserve.[7] These advocacy efforts among domestic workers bring to the forefront the patriarchal, classist, and xenophobic systems that dominate our economies. They demand an end to the invisibilization of the vital work—and the people who carry out that work—that contributes significantly to the functioning of our everyday lives.

In the Catholic tradition, Martha of Bethany is the patron saint of servants and cooks. Despite what I might think about the particularities of Martha's work, I do see her tenacious spirit alive and well in the organizing efforts of domestic workers around the world. Martha is not silent about the workload imbalance in her own home, and neither are the brave individuals who organized and petitioned the ILO. I believe God is working in their midst to bring about a more just economy in which domestic work is appreciated, dignified, and compensated fairly.

AS MUCH as I empathize with Martha, I do wish she would speak with Mary directly instead of putting Jesus in the middle of their conflict. I imagine this sort of dynamic happens regularly, and the resentment Martha feels toward Mary has been building for quite some time. Like my own cycle of resentment, Mary is irritated not only with her sister, but also with her guest. He does nothing to acknowledge the imbalance in their division of labor, nor has he offered to pitch in to help. Martha must feel like he doesn't care a thing about her, and she calls him on it.

This isn't the only instance when Martha has strong words with Jesus. When their brother Lazarus is on his

---

7   Eileen Boris and Jennifer N. Fish. " 'Slaves No More': Making Global Labor Standards for Domestic Workers," Feminist Studies 40: 2 (2014): 411–443.

deathbed, Mary and Martha send word to Jesus to come immediately, but instead of going directly to Bethany, he delays his trip by a couple of days. By the time he arrives Lazarus is dead. Martha confronts him, "Lord, if you had been here, my brother would not have died" (John 11:21). It's hard to argue against that.

These raw, honest moments between Martha and Jesus demonstrate a real depth to their friendship. Open communication in tense situations requires a great deal of trust. I think Martha must know how much Jesus cares for her and her family. Otherwise she wouldn't feel so upset and let down by him.

Honestly, I get frustrated with how Jesus responds to her exasperation: "Martha, Martha, you are worried and distracted by many things; there is need of only one thing. Mary has chosen the better part, which will not be taken from her" (Luke 10:41–42). He could choose to say, "Martha, it sounds like you need a break. Why don't you let me take over for a bit?" Or he could offer to move the conversation he was having with Mary into the space where Martha is working (the kitchen or elsewhere), each of them picking up a piece of the labor. They all could assume the collective doer role, which would lighten Martha's burden. As my daughter loves to sing, "The more we work together the happier we'll be!"

The reality is that, even if what Mary is doing is "better," the work still has to be done by someone. To insist that the daily labor that sustains all of our lives is inferior to and incompatible with the realm of inner spirituality is an assertion rooted in privilege that only reinforces how unfairly we treat those who take on this work, either by choice or necessity.

When I think back to the sermons I've heard on this passage, the implicit message was always that women have to find a way to be Martha and Mary at the same time. As Weaver stresses in her book, we ought to seek the heart of Mary while we function in Martha's world. Be a gracious host and go to whatever lengths you must to provide hospitality, but don't get so caught up in the work that you become snarky with those you are serving. Make sure you spend time in prayer and in studying Scripture — but do that in addition to all of the other tasks on your plate. Achieve perfect balance in all areas of your life, and then you will please God.

Is this really what Jesus is trying to convey to Martha? I don't think so.

Jesus sees that Martha is running herself into the ground. She has taken on the difficult, never-ending work of ministering to others, a challenge he understands well. Even if he and Mary step in to help her, that will only ease her burden momentarily. I don't believe Jesus is telling Martha to take on one more thing and become more "spiritual." He is encouraging her to do *less*.

If Martha continues downs the path of wearing herself out without time for restoration, eventually she will burn out one way or another. I believe Jesus is trying to communicate with his friend that he's worried for her well-being and for the sustainability of her vital ministry, whatever that looks like. *Take care of yourself, Martha.*

Might this story help us unlearn some of our unhealthy patterns about work? Instead of measuring our worthy by the number of hours we spend being productive, could we learn to value time for rest, reflection, and leisure? Could we even see it as holy time?

Mark 5:24b-34

And a large crowd followed him and pressed in on him. Now there was a woman who had been suffering from hemorrhages for twelve years. She had endured much under many physicians, and had spent all that she had; and she was no better, but rather grew worse. She had heard about Jesus, and came up behind him in the crowd and touched his cloak, for she said, "If I but touch his clothes, I will be made well." Immediately her hemorrhage stopped; and she felt in her body that she was healed of her disease. Immediately aware that power had gone forth from him, Jesus turned about in the crowd and said, "Who touched my clothes?" And his disciples said to him, "You see the crowd pressing in on you; how can you say, 'Who touched me?'" He looked all around to see who had done it. But the woman, knowing what had happened to her, came in fear and trembling, fell down before him, and told him the whole truth. He said to her, "Daughter, your faith has made you well; go in peace, and be healed of your disease."

Chapter 9

Heal: The Hemorrhaging Woman

I have a visceral response to being in the same room with well-known people: I want to make a run for it. Whether the person is someone I've never heard of or someone I admire greatly, I maintain a safe distance that allows me to admire them (or not) from afar. You'll never find me waiting outside the backstage doors of a show to catch a performer exit the building. I usually won't even stand in line to have a book signed by its author.

One evening my husband Matt and I drove to the Goodnights Comedy Club in Raleigh, North Carolina to see a stand-up comedian we had watched rise to stardom. The venue only held around a hundred people, and on our way out the door we were surprised to see the comic standing just a few feet away. "Do you want to say hi to him?" Matt asked. I turned and bolted towards the restrooms.

A handful of times I have managed to break from my pattern of avoidance. Several years ago while attending a writing conference I crossed paths with a well-known author who had visited my church a few months earlier. Ever since I'd regretted not having been bolder when she and I were sitting at the same lunch table and unsurprisingly I'd let the opportunity to strike up a conversation pass me by.

This time I decided to risk it despite the awkwardness I felt. Though a bit on the shy side, she couldn't have been kinder as we talked while walking back to our hotel together. My nerves remained, but I mostly kept my composure. As we parted ways I felt a swell of pride. *I did it!*

Moments later I ran into a friend of mine who, in the midst of my recounting what had just happened, looked at my quizzically, touched my arm, and said as politely as she could, "Katey, I think you're wearing your sweater inside out." I felt my cheeks grow hot. Surely the author I'd approached had noticed my fashion mishap as well, but apparently she was too polite to bring it to my attention. I resumed my normal avoid-and-dash routine for the rest of the conference.

I try to imagine what it must be like to be recognizably famous. Getting bombarded constantly by strangers who want something from you—a selfie, a handshake, a favor—must be exhausting. The last thing I want to be is another energy-draining fan.

I'd like to think that my quirky behavior in the presence of notoriety is fairly common. Even so, I wanted to investigate the underlying cause of my inner escape artist. From what I can tell, some combination of empathy and envy is at the root. I've learned that envy can manifest itself in one of two ways: we downplay a person's accomplishments to diminish their success, or we put them on a pedestal in order to distance ourselves.

If Jesus walked among us today, I'd most likely stay home and watch the streaming coverage on Youtube like a modern-day Zacchaeus. Maybe Zacchaeus climbed up the tree, not to get a better glimpse of Jesus, but to keep a safe distance from his power. How many sacred moments have I missed because of my anxiety of the unknown? Am I willing to let my fear stand in the way of an encounter with the divine?

I LONG to embody the bravery of the hemorrhaging woman in the Gospels who risks everything in order to be healed. In the presence of immense power she exudes graceful courage and a tenacious spirit. Her faithful act of reaching out for what she needs—of risking failure and disappointment—is what heals her.

Versions of the hemorrhaging woman's story appear in three of the Gospels—Matthew, Mark, and Luke. The exact nature of her hemorrhaging is unknown, but we can assume that she suffers from some reproductive disorder that causes heavy bleeding, perhaps uterine fibroids or gynecological cancer. Whatever her condition, she suffers both physically and socially. At the time Levitical purity laws regarded menstrual blood as "unclean," and a menstruating woman, along with anything or anyone she touched during her period, was considered unclean for a full seven days after the point of contact (Lev. 15:19—24). All women with regular menstrual cycles would have experienced monthly times of impurity, but this woman is in a constant state of impurity and thus a constant state of social isolation. To be labeled "unclean" restricts the ways in which she is able to move about the world.

Since the bleeding began twelve years ago, she has consulted doctor after doctor in search of a cure. She expends all of her financial resources on treatments but nothing works. In fact, whatever the doctors have prescribed only exacerbates her condition. No matter how diligently she searches for an answer that will bring relief, she can't seem to find a way to stop this flow of blood.

I DON'T KNOW what it's like to live in an environment where my body's natural rhythms dictate where I can and cannot go. During my adolescence, there was a large-scale effort on the part of advertisers to dispel the myth that having a period was a justifiable reason to avoid everyday life. Ads for maxi pads and tampons nearly always featured women and girls wearing form-fitting, light-colored clothing while engaging in sporty activities like rollerblading, swimming, and tennis —and smiling from ear to ear! *With these products, you can forget you're even having a period at all.*

Too many girls in the United States and around the globe don't have the luxury of forgetting about their periods. Buying menstrual management products is a luxury many can't afford, and this lack of access—sometimes referred to as "period poverty"—has real impacts on their lives. Girls may miss up to five days of school each month while menstruating; some eventually drop out altogether. When a girl can't manage her period with dignity, she can't get the education she needs and deserves.

Improving menstruation management begins with ensuring a girl has access to clean water. Worldwide, more than 2.6 billion people live without access to running water, which negatively impacts the entire population but poses particular challenges for menstruating girls.[1] In India, for example, many schools do not have private or

1   World Health Organization, "Meeting the MDG Drinking Water and Sanitation Target: The Urban and Rural Challenge of the Decade," 2006. http://www.who.int.

functioning toilets. Understandably menstruating girls feel uncomfortable using them. On top of that, nearly ninety percent of all menstruating women and girls there do not have access to a regular supply of sanitary pads. As a result, up to twelve percent of all girls in India drop out of school early, either because of the discomfort they feel during their periods or because of how this lack of privacy and sanitary pads impedes their health and dignity.[2]

All girls need access to low-cost or free sanitary supplies, preferably ones that are washable and reusable, to help them manage their periods comfortably. Two companies in Uganda, Afripads and Makapads, are addressing this large unmet need by producing affordable, reusable, and biodegradable pads from locally-sourced materials like papyrus and paper waste. In addition to ensuring girls can stay in school during their periods, these companies also employ hundreds of local women who manage the manufacturing operations.

Girls need more than clean water and affordable hygiene products to manage their periods. They also need a basic understanding of their bodies, puberty, and fertility. Without science-based sexuality education at school or honest, fact-based conversations at home, many girls do not know to expect their periods in the first place. Frightened by the sight of blood, girls may worry that they are sick or dying, or that they have done something wrong. Feeling isolated and ashamed, many girls feel they must hide their periods, even from trusted adults who could assuage their fears by explaining the normal functions of

---

2   WaterAid, "Menstruation should not be taboo. Period." http://www.wateraid.org/news/news/menstruation-should-not-be-taboo.

their bodies.[3]

Girls have yet another reason to hide their periods: menstruation may signal sexual readiness to their communities and thus indicate their marriageability. When a girl marries before she turns eighteen, she is far more likely to become pregnant and give birth before her body has fully developed, and as a result, she is more likely to experience difficulty during labor, which may lead to long-term health complications or even death. One of the most effective strategies we have against the practice of child marriage is keeping girls in school. To ensure girls finish their education, we must ensure that they are learning in safe, supportive environments.

In my research I came across an organization called ZanaAfrica that works specifically with schools in Kenya to supply them with sanitary pads coupled with science-based reproductive health education, including facts about menstruation, for all of their students, girls and boys alike. I love this approach of equipping young people with the information they deserve and the tools they need to live their lives fully and without stigma.

Recently I watched a TED talk given by Aditi Gupta, a social entrepreneur in India who wanted to do something about the social taboos around discussing menstruation in a way that would appeal to young audiences. She created the Menstrupedia Comic: *The Friendly Guide to Periods for Girls*, an illustrated book about puberty, fertility, and menstrual management. Told through story, this comic book provides fun, approachable, and informative lessons

3   Marni Sommer, "Ideologies of sexuality, menstruation and risk: girls' experiences of puberty and schooling in northern Tanzania," Cult Health Sex, May 2009, 11(4): 383–398.

for girls about their reproductive health.

I'm inspired by all of the innovative products and creative strategies that many organizations and individuals are putting into place to ensure every girl has what she needs to finish her education and to live her life with dignity and freedom. How might the church join their efforts to create stigma-free, affirming environments for all of the girls of the world?

WHEN THE BLEEDING WOMAN in the Gospels finds Jesus in the crowd, she is desperate to heal her affliction, to restore her dignity, and to regain her freedom. Worn out, run down, and out of options, she knows his power to heal is her only remaining hope. If she wants to save her life, she has no other choice than to risk taking what she needs.

Making her way through the swarms of people, the woman lowers herself to the ground and begins to crawl on her hands and knees towards Jesus. She decides to approach him from behind in the hopes that she will remain unnoticed and unseen. *I don't need him to see me. I just need to touch him.* Tentatively she extends her arm, her hand inching forward until the moment when her fingertips gently graze the bottom hem of his garment. She senses it immediately. That feather-light touch has stopped her bleeding. Her suffering has ceased.

"Who touched me?" Jesus asks. Her touch has stopped him in his tracks. The disciples are somewhat perturbed by the obviousness of the answer: *You're surrounded by people, Jesus.* But the healed woman knows that he is asking about her. In her attempt to remain unseen, she has underestimated her own power—the power of her faith in Jesus that has catalyzed her miraculous healing.

Not even Jesus knows that it was she who touched him. She has a choice: she can remain silent, or she can risk speaking her truth. With great trepidation she once again makes her way towards Jesus. Falling to her knees, she reveals the story of her suffering and the miracle of her healing. In response to all she has shared, Jesus affirms her: "Daughter, your faith has made you well" (Mark 5:34).

Your faith has made you well. Her belief heals her. Her willingness to keep hope alive, to reach out, to take what she needs to survive—this is what frees her from endless suffering. Her identity is no longer tied to her disease. She is a daughter of God.

May we dare to reach out for healing. May we risk telling our stories of pain and isolation. May our faith ignite the transformation we most desire.

John 20:1-18

Early on the first day of the week, while it was still dark, Mary Magdalene came to the tomb and saw that the stone had been removed from the tomb. So she ran and went to Simon Peter and the other disciple, the one whom Jesus loved, and said to them, "They have taken the Lord out of the tomb, and we do not know where they have laid him." Then Peter and the other disciple set out and went toward the tomb. The two were running together, but the other disciple outran Peter and reached the tomb first. He bent down to look in and saw the linen wrappings lying there, but he did not go in. Then Simon Peter came, following him, and went into the tomb. He saw the linen wrappings lying there, and the cloth that had been on Jesus' head, not lying with the linen wrappings but rolled up in a place by itself. Then the other disciple, who reached the tomb first, also went in, and he saw and believed; for as yet they did not understand the scripture, that he must rise from the dead. Then the disciples returned to their homes.

But Mary stood weeping outside the tomb. As she wept, she bent over to look into the tomb; and she saw two angels in white, sitting where the body of Jesus had been lying, one at the head and the other at the feet. They said to her, "Woman, why are you weeping?" She said to them, "They have taken away my Lord, and I do not know where they have laid him." When she had said this, she turned around and saw Jesus standing there, but she did not know that it was Jesus. Jesus said to her, "Woman, why are you weeping? Whom are you looking for?" Supposing him to be the gardener, she said to him, "Sir, if you have carried him away, tell me where you have laid him, and I will take him away." Jesus said to her, "Mary!" She turned and said to him in Hebrew, "Rabbouni!" (which means Teacher). Jesus said to her, "Do not hold on to me, because I have not yet ascended to the Father. But go to my brothers and say to them, 'I am ascending to my Father and your Father, to my God and your God.'" Mary Magdalene went and announced to the disciples, "I have seen the Lord"; and she told them that he had said these things to her.

Chapter 10

Proclaim: Mary Magdalene

The Spirit of God moves at unexpected times and places. When I spot a single red bloom among the barren trees in wintertime. When I watch my daughter take a bite out of sun-ripened strawberry. When something catches me off guard and pulls my full attention to the present. These breath-taking moments illuminate how Spirit is always at work in my life.

One frigid Saturday morning I took the two-hour train ride from New Haven, Connecticut where I was living at the time to New York City for the day. I'd been invited to join a gathering of advocates working to end gender-based violence. Around a hundred of us made our way to an upper-floor classroom at The New School in Greenwich Village. When we entered the room, most of us were strangers, but in a matter of hours, we managed to form a sacred community of survivors. We took turns sharing our own pain-filled stories of violence, betrayal, survival, and hope. Both gut-wrenching and healing, the act of naming our collective suffering fused us together: our cacophony of individual experiences blended into a unified chorus for justice. What once was hidden had now come into the light.

As we were preparing to close for the day, the song "Walking on Broken Glass" by Annie Lennox suddenly filled the room. Without hesitation or prompting, we all began to dance. I distinctly remember thinking, *I don't care what I look like. I don't care what anyone thinks. I want to dance like no one is watching!* I felt free, uninhibited. For the first time I understood the meaning of the verse "you have turned my wailing into dancing" (Ps. 30:11).

I couldn't tell you how long we danced in that room. It felt like forever—and like a moment. But I remember thinking, *I never want to leave this place.* I longed to soak in the newfound feeling of joyous freedom. Eventually the music died down. It was time for me to catch my train back home. As I walked the twenty blocks back to Grand Central Station, I couldn't quite wrap my mind around what had happened in that room, but I knew that I'd had an unexpected encounter with God and that I would never be the same.

WHEN I THINK about biblical moments of divine surprise, Mary Magdalene's appearance at Jesus's tomb immediately comes to mind. But before I explore that particular story, I want to examine what the Bible says about her life up until that point—and what it *doesn't* say.

In reimagining the stories of biblical women, I have filled in many narrative gaps, strayed far from common interpretations, and offered different, if not controversial perspectives on what their actions and decisions mean. Certainly I've made myriad assumptions along the way. Such readings of Scripture can bring forth new understandings, not only of God's nature, but also of our own lives and beliefs.

There are, however, limitations in reading these sacred texts through our individual lenses. As earnest as our truth-seeking may be, we must remember to refrain from any claims to universality in our readings. What I hope I have conveyed throughout this book is that there is so much we do not and cannot know about these stories. Accepting this gives us permission to imagine what might have been, and it opens us to the movement of the Spirit who uncovers new revelations from the pages of these ancient texts.

One of my seminary professors would say often, "The Bible doesn't *speak*. We interpret it." This concept challenges the notion that a particular interpretation of any biblical text is singularly correct, obviously apparent, and not to be questioned. Not all religious institutions, however, are willing to relinquish the control they have over how certain passages are understood and applied by their followers.

The historic portrayal of Mary Magdalene is a striking example of how biblical interpretation can dictate how communities will read a biblical text for years to come. While male religious authorities largely have ignored the other biblical women I've featured, Pope Gregory the Great discussed Mary Magdalene at length in a 1591 sermon that would shape her legacy for centuries. And the wildest part? He preached from a text that likely has nothing to do with her.

In the seventh chapter of the Gospel of Luke there is a story of an unnamed "sinful" woman who approaches

Jesus with a jar of costly oil. She weeps as she anoints his feet and then wipes them with her hair. It's arguably the most intimate story we have about Jesus's life. There is great power in that intimacy.

In his sermon on the Luke passage, Pope Gregory makes three major logical leaps, steeped in patriarchy, about the unnamed woman in the story—leaps that have absolutely no basis in the text itself. First, he assumes that the sinful woman is a prostitute. (What other "sin" can a woman possibly commit?) Second, he assumes that the unnamed woman is Mary of Bethany. Third, he claims that Mary of Bethany and Mary Magdalene are actually the same person. Even if the first claim is true, the others seem far-fetched. I wonder, could Pope Gregory simply not entertain the real possibility that multiple women play a significant role in Jesus's ministry?

Identifying Mary Magdalene as the nameless sinful woman was an intentional decision. In the biblical accounts Mary has a powerful connection with Jesus. In some ways her relationship with him is closer than the ones he has with his disciples. The fastest way to extinguish a woman's power is to raise questions about her sexuality. These unfounded rumors of Mary's past have overshadowed her significance as the first to witness the resurrected Christ.

Pope Gregory's sermon was not just delivered and forgotten. It became the basis of official Catholic teaching regarding Mary Magdalene. It influenced art and culture for centuries. Even with more recent efforts to refute his claims, they are hard to extract from the broader cultural landscape in which so many depictions of Mary Magdalene as a prostitute exist.

One could argue while this interpretation may be historically inaccurate, there is a certain comfort in picturing someone with a sordid past having a significant role in Jesus's life. If he can welcome a prostitute into his inner circle, then we presumably can have a place there too. I don't deny the power of this inclusion, but it comes at the expense of Mary Magdalene's biblical legacy, namely her role in first proclaiming the Gospel. What if we simply stopped speculating about Mary's sexual past and instead honored her as the first evangelist? Think about what impact that might have on the religious customs and practices that continue to marginalize and minimize women's leadership in our faith communities.

That's why I believe Mary Magdalene gets the patriarchy so riled up in the first place. Her story poses a serious challenge to the male-dominated structures that prevent women from accessing power in the church. Instead of examining these exclusionary teachings and beliefs, male religious leaders have chosen to retell her story in such a way that shifts our attention to questions regarding her sexuality.

The sexualization of women and girls is so widespread today that it makes my head spin. When my daughter was an infant, I came across a picture online of two baby onesies displayed next to each other: one read "I hate my thighs" and the other read "I'm super." I'll let you figure out which one was marketed to parents of baby girls. After public backlash, Wry Baby, the company that created the questionable clothing, begrudgingly took the onesies off store shelves while insisting that "I hate my thighs" was intended to be funny. As the mother of a young girl, I couldn't find anything humorous about producing a fat-shaming message on an article of baby clothing.

From the time they are born, girls are forced to play a game they cannot win. They learn that their access to power lies in their bodies, but only if they are able to conform them to impossible, ever-changing beauty standards rooted in cultural constructions of female desirability. Girls learn that their primary role is to gain the attention of boys and men: to look and act sexy, but not *too* sexy. Sex is something girls are to perform for others (meaning boys and men), not something for their own pleasure or enjoyment. Their bodies are for others to consume, judge, and deem worthy or unworthy.

Too often our faith communities uphold these problematic ideas about women's bodies and their access to power. When we comment on a female pastor's clothing or preach messages of sexual purity to our young girls, we reinforce the systems designed to bar women from using their gifts in church leadership.

We must break free, and Mary Magdalene can help us lead the way.

CONSIDER ALL THAT Mary Magdalene has witnessed since she first encountered Jesus. She has watched the healing work of a man who transformed not only her life, but also the lives of countless others—those ignored, avoided, and ostracized. She believes in the restorative and healing power of his ministry. How shattering, then, for her to stand by helplessly as her teacher and beloved friend is publicly humiliated and brutally executed for his life of loving his community.

She must feel powerless. Devastated. Numb.

On the day of Jesus's murder, there is no space for Mary Magdalene to grieve for her friend. There is no quietness for her mournful cries amidst the sounds of an angry crowd cheering on the torturers and abusers for their own sick pleasure and voyeurism. But she stays. She keeps watch. She remains in that place until the end when Jesus exhales his final shallow breath. *It is finished.*

The summer before my freshman year of high school, a childhood friend of mine died tragically in a car accident. She was a vivacious girl—a tennis superstar, a free spirit, and an awful singer. We registered for the same summer camp in Hendersonville, North Carolina, and on the night of the much-anticipated co-ed dance with a neighboring boys' camp, she'd donned her favorite pair of beat up Air Jordan high tops. Much to my surprise, they were a hit with our male peers. I'd loved—and kind of envied—how she always managed to be authentically herself. I don't think she knew another way.

On the first anniversary of her death I felt pulled to visit her gravesite, but since the burial had been private, I was unsure where to find it in the cemetery. After wandering around aimlessly, I finally approached one of the groundskeepers to ask if she knew where my friend was buried. "Did she happen to love Dr. Pepper?" she asked. I nodded. She then led me down a line of graves near the main road until we'd reached one with a faded can of Dr. Pepper soda next to the headstone. I'd brought with me a single pink rose from the grocery store near the cemetery, and as I leaned down to place it there, I felt somewhat embarrassed by my meager and generic offering. *I should've gotten a new can of Dr. Pepper for you, sweet friend.* Then I wept.

The morning when Mary Magdalene comes to the place where Jesus has been laid to rest, the early light of the sun has yet to break. The world, having returned to its normal rhythms, is still heavy with darkness. But she cannot sleep, not with the harrowing images of his death haunting her dreams. She makes her way alone through the darkness to her friend's tomb where she will present her humble offering of unencumbered grief. There she will give in to the waves of mourning as they crash over her again and again.

Her plans to grieve in the solitude of night are thwarted by a stunning discovery: the stone that had been placed in front of Jesus's place of burial is no longer there. She seeks the help of some of the disciples who confirm what she most fears: the body is gone.

Mary feels compelled to enter the empty tomb herself. As she peers inside the lightless space, she encounters two angels standing by Jesus's burial garment. But then a voice calls out to her from beyond the grave: "Woman, why are you weeping?" She peers outside, her eyes unable to make out the figure shrouded in darkness. *It must be the gardener.* But then he speaks her name. With the utterance of a single word the impossible has been made possible. Jesus is not dead. He is here. He is alive. He knows her name.

Only a handful of days have passed since Mary's heart was ripped open by the violent murder of her friend. She has come to the grave to grieve only to discover that his body is gone. She is beyond devastated, and her grief is compounded. But in an instant, her weeping is transformed into dancing when she hears him speak her name. She must want to stay in that place with him forever. But Jesus has other plans for her. *Go and tell what you have seen.*

Like Mary Magdalene, each of us is called to be witnesses to the ways that God brings forth life from death. In our sharing of these resurrection moments, we become the bearers of hope through which community is formed, truth is revealed, and lives are redeemed.

Jesus chooses Mary Magdalene to be the first witness of the resurrection. As his beloved friend, he knows that she is both trustworthy and qualified to speak the truth of what she has seen and heard. *Go proclaim the Gospel.*

Speaking our truth takes courage. Many people would rather not hear our truth, especially if what we have to say disrupts the status quo and demands a change.

We've seen this time and time again in the lives of biblical women who struggle to have their voices recognized and their stories told. We know it from our own experiences as well. *Women, be silent in churches.*

But we will not be silenced. We will not deny what we have seen—the places where God is bringing forth new life, the places where God is calling us to bear witness to the truth of death-conquering love.

We will be like Mary Magdalene in our truth-telling.

We will usher in a new era of justice, kindness, and mercy.

We will rise up.

Conclusion

Hagar. Rachel. Shiphrah. Puah. Moses's mother. Hannah. Ruth. The widow with oil. Mary. Martha. The hemorrhaging woman. Mary Magdalene.

These women have been my spiritual guides and faithful companions over these last few years. I've cried with Hannah in the temple. I've wandered in the wilderness with Hagar. I've carried the burden of an undervalued workload with Martha. I've witnessed God's presence in the most unexpected of places with Mary Magdalene.

Each of their stories challenges my thinking about what it means to follow God. They disrupt my tendency to seek easy answers to life's most complex questions. They remind me that our struggles for justice today are tied to an ancient history of oppression and resistance.

As I've come to know these women, I have felt Spirit's movement within me, bringing forward new questions to explore: How do I honor their stories in my own life? How do I honor their legacy in my advocacy work for women and girls?

Working on this book has moved me into new places of understanding of God's calling for my life. Though my sense of purpose has not changed, the ways in which I feel drawn to live that out in my daily life are ever-evolving. I find myself returning to these same texts again and again in search of new revelations and insights. This is what it means for the text to be living.

May we continue to search for sacred stories of resistance—in the Bible, in the world, and in our own lives. May we honor them with our words, our prayers, and our actions. May we rise with them to meet the challenges of today's struggle for a more just, compassionate world.

May it be so.

Made in the USA
Middletown, DE
09 January 2021